Do It Yourself
Guide to
BIODIESEL

Do It Yourself Guide to

BIODIESEL

YOUR ALTERNATIVE FUEL SOLUTION FOR

- ## SAVING MONEY

- ## REDUCING OIL DEPENDENCY

- ## HELPING THE PLANET

GUY PURCELLA

Ulysses Press

Published by: Ulysses Press
P.O. Box 3440
Berkeley, CA 94703
www.ulyssespress.com

ISBN10: 1-56975-624-4
ISBN13: 978-1-56975-624-9
Library of Congress Control Number: 2007905319

Printed in Canada by Webcom

10 9 8 7 6 5 4 3 2

Contributing writer: Beth Ann Petro Roybal
Acquisitions editor: Nick Denton-Brown
Managing editor: Claire Chun
Editor: Mark Woodworth
Proofreader: Elyce Petker
Editorial and production: Lauren Harrison, Judith Metzener
Index: Sayre Van Young
Cover design: Double R Design
Interior design and layout: what!design @ whatweb.com

Distributed by Publishers Group West

TO MY LOVING WIFE, SHERIE
TO MY FATHER AND MOTHER
AND TO MY CLOSE FRIEND HEATHER

TABLE OF CONTENTS

ACKNOWLEDGMENTS

I would like to thank my loving, supporting wife for all her support through the hard times, the long nights at the computer, and the thousands of hours I've spent reading books, watching shows about the ecology, and scouring the Internet in my unrelenting thirst for knowledge about alternative energy sources, especially biodiesel. Thank you for providing that balance in my life that everyone needs. You are a blessing not just to me, but to those who know you or get to share a brief moment with you. You've inspired many others to overcome their hardships. You've always supported my decision to write this book and to start a business selling biodiesel equipment.

I also want to thank my father, George, for encouraging me to build our first biodiesel processor, and for inspiring me to learn about something that I now feel tremendous excitement about. You've patiently stood by me while we learned about biodiesel together, and never got tired of listening to me. I finally found a direction in my life, something that I believe in wholeheartedly, and I thank you for supporting me in my decision.

I want to thank my mother, Barbara, for being a loving, kind person who has always been there for me. It is perhaps she who is most responsible for my having the time to write this book. Thank you for the wonderful memories in our life, for helping to guide me through life, and for all you've done. I'm a very lucky person to have two parents who are both so loved by those around them, and especially by me. (Yes, Mom, I'll buy you that new TV now.)

My grateful thanks to my close friend, my confidante, and my other mother, Heather, who has been an amazing friend to me and has helped me so many times that I wouldn't know where to start acknowledging it. It's nice to be such good friends with someone who's your stepmother (but more like a second mother to me) and a best friend.

Special thanks to my business associates, especially Noel, for holding the assembly and shipping operation together under some trying times. You've all stuck it out the whole time, and I thank you all. Thanks also to John and Pat for your help with the books, payroll, and other business activities. I believe in the saying "Do what you love, and the necessary resources will follow." So thank you for your help while I do what I love.

Finally, thanks to my sister, Laura, and brothers, Marty and Zane, and all our friends and family for their support and help in my life. I've been so involved in my business venture and in writing this book that I've haven't gotten to spend much time with everyone. So thank you for understanding why Guy has been staying home a lot to work on his biodiesel book or the EZBiodiesel website. Don't be surprised to see more of me soon!

PREFACE

Your first questions when considering this book will likely be, "Why should I choose this book over the others out there?" And "What makes the author qualified to write a book about biodiesel?" Let me take a minute to answer.

First off, this book is not meant to be a theoretical, definitive, scientific analysis. Instead, it's intended as a guide to help the average person learn the basics of what biodiesel is and how to make it at home, as well as a source for some advanced techniques and theories. I'll discuss the benefits and drawbacks of biodiesel along with the environmental and financial reasons that it may be the best alternative fuel available today. (The Introduction will cover these in detail.) While you don't have to be a chemist to make and understand biodiesel, you do have to understand the proper techniques to make high-quality fuel while avoiding problems in the process. I've written this book with that in mind, and I offer many tips and tricks to make things smoother along the way.

I've been interested in alternative energy for many years now. The idea of producing energy of some sort from "free" sources like the sun, water, and wind—and even from "waste" products such as used motor oil—has always intrigued me. So when I first heard about biodiesel, and how I could actually make a high-quality diesel fuel at home, out of free waste cooking oil, for less

than $1 a gallon, I was hooked.

The idea of making my own fuel really piqued my curiosity. I was getting fed up with rising fuel costs and the greed of the big oil companies. I was especially sick of knowing how much of our money was going to rich foreign oil cartels and how many wars we fight to protect our oil interests

AUTHOR FILLING UP WITH BIODIESEL

abroad. I decided to build my own fuel processor so that I could begin making homemade biodiesel myself. "How hard could it be?" I asked myself. It wasn't long until I realized I had a lot to learn about the process, the science of it, and other factors.

Although my first batch of biodiesel came out more or less OK, I knew I had to delve much more deeply into the subject. So I began reading everything I could to learn all about biodiesel—from sources on the Internet, from the available books and journal articles, and so on. I was intent on learning all I could to make the highest-quality fuel possible. After all, my family and I would be using it in newer vehicles that would be quite costly to repair if we damaged the engine with our homemade fuel. In the course of my study, I read many first-person accounts from others who had engine problems from using low-grade biodiesel. These usually were the result of improper processing procedures, outdated techniques, skipping of important steps, and the like. So I decided to find out how to avoid those problems, profit from others' mistakes, and seek out exactly what it took to make clean, reliable biodiesel for myself.

Because the available information was so scattered, and extremely difficult to decipher, I finally decided to tackle writing this book. I realized there wasn't a really good book on the market that would help the average person understand biodiesel and how it's made. So I dug in, and spent about a thousand hours reading forums, websites, books, and manuals. It turned out to be quite difficult to weed out the theoretical, unproven techniques from the tried-and-true methods. I wanted to greatly simplify the process for everyone else and compile in one book all the most current, proven, and safe information about making biodiesel. I also wanted to create an easy reference guide, plus a complete index, which would make it easier to find information when needed. Finally, I wanted to pass on all the tips and tricks I learned over the past two years of making biodiesel, saving my readers the frustration of learning them on their own—the hard way.

In this book you'll find a lot of current information (presented in clear, ordinary terms) that you won't find anywhere else— what biodiesel is and how it's made, important tips and tricks for processing it, lists of items needed for titration, how to do test batches, the best ways of oil collection, and so on. This book will also give you many ideas on how to stay up-to-date with current procedures and information, such as websites to visit and books to read. Much of it is information my colleagues and I learned in the process of making biodiesel ourselves, in manufacturing and selling our own line of EZBiodiesel™ processors on our website (*www.ezbiodiesel.com*), and in studying the vast amount of public information available. We've been putting that information to rigorous use, along with testing and retesting many ideas of our own. There's a lot of outdated, merely theoretical, and inaccurate information out there, so you'll save a *lot* of time by using this book.

Since our humble beginning of building a few processors in our garage, we have now evolved into a company offering more than 10 models of biodiesel processors and DIY (do-it-yourself) kits, which we build in our manufacturing facility. We have models that range from those that will produce as little as 20 gallons per batch, to several commercial versions capable of producing over 1 million gallons a year or more. We're expanding operations as this book is going to press, and we expect to become a full-service, alternative energy business offering all forms of alternative energy, in addition to biodiesel.

Since writing my initial version of this book (which was sold on our website, without having to advertise it at all), I have successfully used our homemade biodiesel in my own 2003 GMC

ONE OF FOUR DIESEL VEHICLES THAT AUTHOR'S FAMILY RUNS ON BIODIESEL

Duramax, my family's 2002 and 2006 Duramax engines, and a 2007 Cummins engine, plus our new 2007 Massey Ferguson tractor—all with great results. Between all my family members, we have currently driven about 50,000 miles using mostly B100 (100 percent biodiesel), though we run B50 or less (50 percent biodiesel) in the winter in our cold Colorado climate.

Methods of making biodiesel at home or in your small business are constantly evolving, with new techniques, useful tips, and tricks being discovered and refined all the time. Making biodiesel yourself has recently attracted huge interest around the world, due to rising and unpredictable fuel prices, the ongoing wars over oil, a variety of challenging environmental concerns, and the realization that our oil supplies are quickly dwindling. In addition, many people find great satisfaction in making their own homemade biodiesel while saving a huge amount of money.

In his book *Out of Gas: The End of the Age of Oil*, David Goodstein makes a strong argument that worldwide production of oil will peak soon, possibly within this decade.[1] That will be followed by declining availability of fossil fuels that could plunge the world into global conflicts as nations struggle to capture a share of shrinking oil

= Oil Consumption & Price

reserves. And, of course, fuel prices will skyrocket (they reached historic highs in 2006, and did so again in October 2007, with oil at over $93 per barrel, even as this book was being finished, carried higher and higher by tight supplies, Mideast turmoil, and speculative trading). The good news is that each one of us can help reduce our collective dependence on foreign oil through using alternative fuels and exploring the use of other energy sources. We can consider alternatives such as ethanol, electric hybrid cars, hydrogen-fueled cars, and so on.

But right now, in my view, biodiesel is one of the *very best alternatives,* because of its many benefits. This book will tell you all about it.

HOW TO USE THIS BOOK

I have presented the information in this book in a logical order, both to make it easier to understand and to help you find information later for reference as you start making your own biodiesel. A few hints and tips will help you get the most out of this book.

First, though, I strongly suggest that you **read this entire book before you begin** trying to make a large batch of biodiesel. There are a few sections you could skip for now, but read most of it *first*, then try making a minibatch. I'm sure that you're excited and eager to make your first batch, but if you rush into it too soon, you may make mistakes (or failed batches). And *even if it looks good*, you may have done something wrong and not even know it. Often a batch of biodiesel can look fine to the naked eye but still contain impurities that may cause damage to your vehicle over time. Although it's not likely that one or two tankfuls alone will damage your engine, it is possible that, as time goes by, you will have problems with low-grade biodiesel—so why take the chance?

So please take time to read the entire book, which will help you understand the process, how it works, and why. Of course, everyone will encounter different challenges when making biodiesel, and I can't possibly cover them all here. If you understand the process well, however, you'll be better able to adapt your situation to still produce high-quality biodiesel with the fewest problems.

As I present the information in this book, I will sometimes use terms that you may not yet understand or be familiar with. If that's the case, I will usually define the term right then. If you need more help, refer to the Glossary section at the back of the book. If you forget what something means over the course of your reading, go to the Glossary for a reminder.

Also, be sure to check out the Further Learning and Resources section at the back for additional ways to further your knowledge of biodiesel (including websites and forums, as well as sources for chemicals and so on). Making biodiesel is an ever-evolving process, and you'd do well to continue to stay abreast of developments.

Keep an eye out, too, for Tips and Notes boxes. These contain useful bits of information that can help you better understand the material you're currently reading.

I've also created a special webpage for all buyers of this book, which contains additional color photos, clickable website links, links to biodiesel-related items for sale, and much more. You can access this page at: *www.ezbiodiesel.com/bookbonus.htm.*

If you plan on making a test batch, or even a larger batch, use the Shopping List Worksheet at the back of the book. Make some copies of the blank worksheet and then every time you read about an item that you might need, simply write it on your list. I've started one list to give you some ideas.

My final piece of advice is this: Consider purchasing a preassembled processor or a do-it-yourself kit from a reputable processor manufacturer, instead of trying to design and build your own from scratch. The reason is that *very few* readers will have any experience in making biodiesel. And even if you do have some experience, chances are good that you've made a low grade of biodiesel and didn't even realize it, unless you have spent many hundreds of hours studying the process. The bottom line is that there's more to designing a processor than simply getting the fluids to flow where you want them.

If you have any doubts at all about your ability to design an effective system, your safest bet for avoiding damage to your vehicle is to purchase a system from a reputable vendor. Yet if you read and study this book carefully, and if your mechanical skills are good, you *can* build your own biodiesel processor, though you should be prepared to rebuild your design several times before you get it right. Expect dozens of trips to hardware stores, visits to Internet sites, long nights and weekends in the garage, and so forth. Yes, it can be exasperating to build your own, but in the end it will be worth it—only if you have the skills and patience. Even if you purchase a ready-made unit, you'll get the same satisfaction of knowing you're burning a fuel you made yourself, and one that is much better for the environment, your engine, and our country. Either way, you need to fully understand the information presented in this book before making your own biodiesel.

WHY BIODIESEL? AND IS IT FOR YOU?

"Our plan is to fuel the future with renewable fuel 'alternatives.' Increased biodiesel usage marks the beginning of a major shift toward sustainability and improved health in our community and beyond."
—RAY NEWKIRK, COFOUNDER AND PRESIDENT, PACIFIC BIOFUELS, INC.

You know that yellow stuff you put on your hot dog (or soy dog) on the 4th of July? Someday soon you could also be putting mustard into your fuel tank as well. Using biodiesel produced from locally grown crops like mustard is certainly a patriotic act—and it's easier on the environment, it's economic, and it builds stronger communities, too. Here's how it works with the mustard crop: Santa Cruz area farmer Ken Kimes and other farmers along California's central coast are growing mustard, which is easier to refine than the most commonly used source of biodiesel, soybeans. A nearby biofuels manufacturer then processes the harvested mustard seed. The resulting biodiesel is distributed by Pacific Biofuels to coastal California diesel owners, including individual drivers, commercial fleets, farmers, and bus companies. The local connection not only results in an environmentally friendly fuel, but also limits environmental damage and extra costs associated with transporting the seeds elsewhere for processing and then back again for distribution. Even better, the leftovers from processing the mustard seed can be used as an herbicide.[2]

Mustard seed oil is a great example of the possibility of biofuels. One of the reasons biodiesel, in particular, is so exciting is that it can be made fairly easily from many renewable, locally grown crops. And, if you find a local source of oil (such as that Chinese restaurant down the street), you can make biodiesel yourself.

Believe it or not, the concept of biodiesel isn't new. The man who invented the diesel engine in 1892—Rudolf Diesel—intended his "baby" to run on a variety of fuel sources, including peanut oil. What happened? Why were biofuels relegated to the history books for so long? Why did petroleum come to the fore, instead? Let's take a closer look at some of the history surrounding the use of petroleum-based fuels, including social, economic, and political implications. Then we'll review the available alternatives. Finally, we'll talk about ways to make and use biodiesel, and why it makes sense both personally and globally.

Did You Know? It takes 10 tons of mustard seed to make 800 gallons of biodiesel.

THE PROBLEM WITH OIL

"The tripling of oil prices since 1998 alone has significantly worsened poverty and environmental damage. Too poor to afford oil and gas, hundreds of millions of people around the world have no choice but to cut trees for heating and cooking. This damages the biosphere, while wasting humanity's time and health."

—WADI'H HALABI, *PEOPLE'S WEEKLY WORLD NEWSPAPER*[3]

Early motorized vehicles were designed for a variety of fuels: steam, diesel, gasoline, and even electric. What happened? In the United States, discovery of huge sources of oil led the push toward inexpensive, petroleum-based fuels. The short story: gasoline and diesel were cheap. Even as late as 1995, experts saw no end to the supply of any of the products provided by nature. As economics professor Julian Simon put it then, "Technology exists now to produce in virtually inexhaustible quantities just about all the products made by nature.... We have in our hands now...the technology to feed, clothe and supply energy to an ever-growing population for the next seven billion years."[4]

Times—and perspectives—sure have changed! Today, fossil fuels represent an increasingly expensive and unavailable option at all levels: individuals, communities, societies, countries, and the entire

world. Oil prices have tripled since 1998.[5] The cost you pay at the
pump, along with other less-obvious costs, makes the continued
reliance on fossil fuels an exorbitant proposition. Besides leaving an
obvious dent in your wallet, fossil fuels also cause massive damage
to the environment, create economic stagnation, and cause terrible
political and social upheaval. Let's take a closer look at these costs
as the first step in putting the viability of biodiesel into context.

Just a Note: In this section, we'll use the terms "fossil fuels,"
"petroleum," and "oil" interchangeably, unless stated
otherwise.

DAMAGE TO THE ENVIRONMENT

Hurricanes that routinely reach deadly Category 5 status. Melting
glaciers causing ocean levels to rise higher each year. Average
temperatures breaking new records every year—leading to hundreds
of deaths. Persistent droughts lasting more than a few years in
areas where they were previously infrequent. Increased flooding in
other areas because of excessive rainfall. All these "natural"
disasters have a common cause: global warming caused by the
burning of fossil fuels. Global warming is primarily a result of
excess levels of carbon dioxide that build up in our atmosphere,
creating an invisible "blanket" that traps heat as it tries to escape
the atmosphere. According to U.S. Department of Energy projections,
worldwide levels of carbon dioxide (CO_2) emissions will rise 60
percent from 1999 to 2020, primarily caused by burning fossil
fuels.[6] Increased CO_2 levels are a major factor behind the
"greenhouse effect," leading to global warming. Other pollutants
from fossil fuels, like carbon monoxide, sulfur dioxide, and
hydrocarbons, cause harm as well.[7,8]

Most experts now agree that global warming is real. The effects
are being felt already. Take a look at these U.S. statistics from
Environmental Defense:[9]

— 2006 was the hottest year on record in the U.S.
— The U.S. fire season has increased by 78 days over the past 20 years.
— The U.S. ranks #1 for global warming pollution

Other countries face similar changes due to global warming.

What are the consequences of this climatic change? Among the
most severe are increased temperatures, which can lead to changing

weather patterns, resulting in droughts, floods, and rising sea levels. It's estimated that these weather disruptions could force up to 200 million people worldwide to become displaced by 2080.[10] Scientists suggest that the U.S. needs to decrease global warming pollution 80 percent by 2050 in order to prevent the most catastrophic consequences for the world.[11] That's a tall order to fulfill.

Did You Know? Petroleum-based diesel fuel is one of the primary culprits responsible for environmental damage. In the U.S., vehicles burned 36 billion gallons of diesel in 2002, for example. That's enough diesel to fill up the entire Great Lakes seven times![12]

ECONOMIC STAGNATION

For decades, cheap oil has been the driving force behind the economic development of just about every country. From fuel to fertilizers to plastics, petroleum and other fossil fuels form the essential ingredients that make our way of life possible, in many respects. Our reliance on oil stems from an implicit belief that we *need* it and that it is in *unlimited* supply. This has led to attitudes of entitlement and complacency, especially in the U.S. where we often feel that our tradition of political, economic, and individual freedoms grants us implicit right to possess anything we can put our hands on—including oil.

Two problems result as our expectations bump up against the realities. First, we have become totally dependent on oil-based products in almost every aspect of our lives. And second, oil supplies are *not* unlimited. Many experts predict that peak oil production is imminent.

OUR DEPENDENCE ON OIL

One way to understand how dependent we are on oil is to think about what it might be like if we didn't have access to it. Imagine what might happen if petroleum and related products became unavailable to farmers. Here's a scenario to consider: Farmer John goes out to his field one day, ready to get to work—but without his usual reliance on oil. The first problem is obvious: How is he going to run his tractor and other farm equipment? Maybe he's lucky and

Jay Leno and Biodiesel: More Than a Good Story

At the Specialty Equipment Marketing Association convention in 2006, comedian and talk show host Jay Leno unveiled the latest car in his extensive collection, a jet-engine, biodiesel-powered car.[57] His "EcoJet" was created by General Motors and was designed to maintain "supercar" (think "very fast") status while at the same time following all the rules for creating an ecologically sensitive vehicle. "Hopefully the rear is what most people will see," quipped Leno. "Fast, safe, sexy, beautiful...and also green," is the summary of Frank Saucedo of the GM design studio. Admittedly, its fuel mileage isn't great, but Leno believes that the renewable source of fuel makes up for the low mpg. You can't find the EcoJet at your local GM dealer, but Leno hopes that GM and other car manufacturers will take what they've learned and apply it to making more environmentally friendly vehicles for the average guy or gal.

has a horse or two in the back pasture that he can hook up to a rusty plow belonging to his great-grandparents that was formerly used as a yard decoration. But think of how long it's going to take him to plow that field by himself. And he also needs to feed the horses part of what he grows in order to keep them healthy and strong enough to continue working. Then there are the fertilizers and pesticides he normally uses to keep the crops growing well, free of weeds and insects. Guess what those items are made of? Oil. Without these products, his crop yield is down. When the crop is finally harvested, how will Farmer John transport it to market? Now imagine this same scenario being repeated, farm by farm, across the country, and you'll see how devastating it could be when oil supplies continue to decrease. Throw in a few other routine problems faced by farmers, such as drought or too much rain, and it wouldn't take much for the entire food supply to be completely disrupted—all stemming from no oil.[13]

Now for a real-world example: North Korea. In the 1990s when the Soviet Union fell apart, North Korea lost its key supporter, leaving the country without means to acquire oil products (the country has no oil or gas supply of its own). Only about 20 percent of the nation's agricultural equipment was still in use by the end of the 1990s, and soil became depleted as fertilizers were not available to replace nutrients. Although many more people took jobs in agriculture, production was still down, contributing to a continuing downward spiral of the economy.[14]

Did You Know? We use oil to fuel our vehicles and generate electricity, though we're dependent on oil in other ways, too. Consider these examples:[15]

- The food on each U.S. dinner plate travels an average of 1,300 miles (in oil-fueled vehicles) to get there.
- It takes about 7 gallons of oil to make 1 tire.
- Most fertilizers and pesticides are made from oil.
- 90 percent of organic (carbon-based) chemicals come from oil, including chemicals used for medicine, cosmetics, plastics, and computers.

A DECREASING SUPPLY OF OIL

Is it true that oil is running out? Most experts say, "yes." Up until recently, oil was relatively easy to extract: Dig a deep hole and pump out the oil. This method has worked quite well for many decades. But the "easy," conventional oil is harder to find, while demand for oil is still growing, particularly in rapidly expanding economies like those of China and India. The same is true for natural gas. For example, natural gas production continues to decline throughout North America.[16] The ground in North America and throughout the rest of the world still holds a lot more oil and gas, but it is mixed with sand, tar, or soft rock. Canada's enormous land contains great areas of oil sands, Venezuela has a vast tar belt, Madagascar and Saudi Arabia contain heavy oil, and Texas has extensive gas shale deposits.[17] Yet getting it out and processing it is more difficult, more damaging to the environment, and more expensive.

Energy industry investment banker Matthew Simmons sums up the problems this way: "The ability to extract this heavy oil in significant volumes is still non-existent.... Worse, it takes vast quantities of scarce and valuable potable water and natural gas to turn unusable oil into heavy low-quality oil.... In a sense, this exercise is like turning gold into lead."[18]

The world's large energy companies are rushing to invest in the attempt to "turn gold into lead," by purchasing interests in unconventional sources, along with natural gas, in an attempt to meet the growing demand for fossil fuels. The name of the game still seems to be finding ways to meet demand through mining more fossil fuel, whatever the cost. And demand for fossil fuels is definitely rising—

dramatically—despite individual attempts at conservation or seeking alternative technologies and fuel sources. From 1999 to 2020, energy demand throughout the world is expected to have increased by 59 percent, according to the U.S. Department of Energy.[19] But U.S. oil reserves are expected to be depleted by 2015. The most optimistic worldwide prediction states that world oil reserves will last only until 2045.[20] Many experts believe that the peak in oil production is occurring now.[21] Whether the date is now, 2015, or 2045, the date of peak oil production is imminent. And from that point on, world citizens will be using more oil than can be pumped out of the ground.

Severe economic consequences and their social ramifications are already starting to be felt and may continue to steadily worsen. In the U.S. over the last few years, you'll find most people grumbling at the sharp increases in the cost of gasoline and diesel that they've pumped into their vehicles—and perhaps that's even why you picked up this book, in an attempt to find a more cost-effective solution for fuel. At an individual level, increased energy prices *do* take a greater chunk of change at a time when other costs such as housing are also steadily increasing. But there's more. Fossil fuels such as coal, oil, and natural gas are used for generating electricity and creating thousands of products that we use unthinkingly each day: household plastics, pharmaceuticals and cosmetics, fabrics, fertilizers, composites used in furniture, flooring, other building supplies, and more.

CONFRONTING OUR ECONOMIC DEPENDENCE ON OIL

How on earth did we become so completely dependent on a resource that is getting to be more difficult and dangerous to obtain? The obvious answer is that oil companies carry enormous political and economic clout. Up until recently, it was not perceived to be in their best interests to encourage the careful stewardship of our resources. Yet there's more to it than that. Whether you chalk it up to problems inherent in market capitalism or plain old individual selfishness, the fact is that we want what we want—and up until now, oil has made it easy to get what we want without worrying too much about the impact on anyone else. Throw in other factors such as the continuing growth of world population, and it's no surprise that we're facing an energy crisis of unprecedented magnitude. Which leads to another problem with oil: political and social upheaval.

POLITICAL AND SOCIAL UPHEAVAL

"After days of shortages in Nepal, the state-owned petroleum importer and distributor finally reached the minimum mandatory level of fuel stocks and stopped delivering supplies to gas stations."

—ASSOCIATION FOR THE STUDY OF PEAK OIL AND GAS (ASPO),

PEAK OIL REVIEW, JULY 9, 2007[22]

Fuel shortages; terrorists blowing up pipelines; farmers thrown off their land; fighting between neighbors, states, and countries; and widespread electricity blackouts. These events aren't mere speculation about "what if" we run out of oil. These events are happening *now*—because of oil. Exploring for, extracting, processing, and using fossil fuels has always had political and social implications. However, unless you've lived right where the action was, you may not be aware of the social and political downside of our dependence on oil. As oil becomes more difficult to obtain, social and political problems become more obvious to all of us.

War is one social and political outcome of our thirst for oil. Ever since oil was discovered, it seems to have gone hand-in-hand with conflict. The Iraq war isn't the first war fought over oil—and it's not likely to be the last. Few countries, including the U.S., will admit that the need for oil is the primary impetus for what is euphemistically termed "protecting our interests" throughout the world. However, "resource security in the Middle East" is part of Australia's stated defense strategy, to name just one country, and its justification for becoming involved in the war in Iraq. One of the consequences of oil-based conflicts—and even the simple exploration, drilling, and processing of oil—is the disruption of people's lives.

Other examples of the social and political consequences of oil shortages, exploration, mining, and processing abound—though you rarely hear about them on the daily news reports on TV. The group Environmental Defense points to the Chad–Cameroon oil and pipeline project as a prime example of oil projects gone horribly wrong.[23] When the project was approved in 2000, the World Bank declared that the project would use oil wealth to directly benefit the poor, with little environmental damage. ExxonMobil headed up the efforts. The result so far? Residents have become even poorer as their land was taken. Many haven't been compensated for the loss of land and livelihood. New workers have flooded the area seeking jobs, stressing health care and other systems. Risk for malaria, AIDS, and other diseases has increased. Water has become polluted and wildlife is disappearing.

Chad and Cameroon aren't the only places experiencing social, economic, and political consequences associated with oil. Rolling blackouts lasting for a few hours or even days are common in Iraq and Nigeria. Gambia has considered stopping all electricity production because the country is unable to afford the fuel needed to generate power. Attacks on oil drilling rigs and kidnappings are common in the Niger Delta oil area. In Argentina, severe shortages in natural gas have led to rationing. In China, an estimated 750,000 people die prematurely each year from air pollution caused by burned fossil fuel. In Russia, Parliament has granted one oil company the right to employ armed guards. In Iran, black-market fuel costs seven times the legal price. And even here in the U.S., refinery slowdowns have created fuel shortages for truck drivers in North Dakota and elsewhere. These events are culled from just one week's news review from ASPO.[24] From North Dakota to Iran, every day people are suffering the social and economic consequences of growing shortages and rising costs of oil and oil-related products.

WHAT ARE THE ALTERNATIVES TO OIL?

Finding ways to reduce the problems associated with oil requires ending our dependence on this limited resource. But how? Efforts focus on three areas:
— Understanding the role of oil in all aspects of our lives, personally and globally
— Changing the way we use oil
— Finding alternatives to oil

UNDERSTANDING OIL'S PLACE IN OUR LIVES

Understanding the role of oil in our lives can be difficult and disheartening. It's a process that occurs over time. One way to get started is to understand the true cost of the fuel and other oil-related products we use every day. U.S. Representative Tom Udall points to the costs—social, economic, and environmental—that go beyond what we pay at the pump—and that are more than double the 40 cents or so worth of per-gallon federal and state fuel taxes.[25] First is the full cost of road maintenance. Government groups at all levels use much more than the taxes they collect from fuel to fund building and fixing our roads. Then there are the health and environmental costs resulting from air pollution. These costs find their way to higher out-of-pocket health care costs, high health insurance premiums, and rising numbers of people—especially children and older adults—with respiratory illnesses such as asthma. Environmental costs include funds spent researching and stemming the loss of wildlife and habitat, as well as financial burdens created by cleaning up oil-related accidents such as oil spills. The taxes associated with the sale of fuel do nothing to address the costs associated with global warming, such as disaster relief for people suffering the adverse effects of drought, hurricanes, or floods resulting from global warming–induced changes in weather patterns. Finally, fuel taxes don't account for costs associated with the threats to our country's security rising from importing oil. These costs include the high cost of fighting wars in areas where we wish to protect our access to oil. Udall also maintains that because citizens don't see the "true" cost of oil, there is little incentive for private investment in alternative technologies and fuels.[26] Oil-based products are essentially subsidized, competing (with an unfair advantage) against alternatives. Although petroleum companies benefit from this in the short-run, we all lose in the end.

CHANGING THE WAY WE USE OIL

Once we understand the role of oil in our world, its true cost, and its impact on our lives locally and globally, then we can begin to change the way we view and use oil. These changes range from small to large, from short-term to long-term. In the long run it may mean reconfiguring our way of living. This concept isn't new—just frequently overlooked. When speaking of the oil crisis in the 1970s, President Jimmy Carter stated, "We must face the prospect of changing our basic ways of living. This change will either be made on our own initiative in a planned way, or forced on us with chaos and suffering by the inexorable laws of nature."[27] Now many folks are wishing they had paid more attention to Carter rather than continuing with our nonstop "use it or lose it" attitude.

While it's inevitable that in the long run our society will need to develop new attitudes and approaches to energy use, providing alternatives to oil itself is a good short-term strategy. That's where the whole idea of alternative fuels like biodiesel comes in: Swap out oil-based products, and swap in alternatives. Of course, it's not as easy as it sounds. Some alternatives require dramatic changes in the vehicles we use—such as using solar or wind power, or using hydrogen fuel cells. Over the long-term, solutions that require major changes in technology are likely to play a role in solving many energy needs—including those of transportation, but this will require new attitudes, new vehicles, and a lot of imagination to implement.[28] Most importantly, these alternatives require time— time we just may not have.

UNDERSTANDING LIMITATIONS OF ALTERNATIVE FUELS

Other seemingly safe alternatives create a whole unexpected set of problems. Take biofuels, for example. Biofuels are fuels created from any sort of vegetation—called biomass.[29] One biofuel, ethanol, is currently made mostly from corn. As a result, the price of corn worldwide has skyrocketed.[30] From U.S. ranchers looking for corn to feed their cattle, to Mexican citizens simply trying to buy tortillas, people all over the world are feeling the pinch. On top of the corn shortage, at least one researcher has suggested that it takes a lot more energy to make corn into ethanol than the resulting energy produced by the ethanol—sort of a 2 + 2 = 3 scenario.[31] Not an efficient way to create energy! Interestingly, one possible solution is to use byproducts of biofuel production—such as distiller's grains from ethanol and byproduct glycerine from biodiesel—as cattle and poultry feed.[32] Researchers are also discovering that other plants, such as the native prairie switchgrass, may be even more effective in making ethanol.

Other alternative fuel "swaps" are more straightforward. The benefit of these kinds of changes is that they can be somewhat easier, perhaps also less costly, than rethinking the entire relationship between oil and ourselves. Another benefit is that you can begin making changes immediately. These fuel alternatives may "buy time" for long-term changes to develop. The downside is that, in some cases, providing alternatives may not address underlying issues, such as people commuting long distances between work and home or our unthinking need for plastic-based disposables.

For any short-term alternative fuel, the goals include the following:
— Renewability and sustainability
— Friendly "footprint" on the earth, including little impact on the environment throughout the process of creating, producing, and using the fuel
— Reasonable cost
— Able to be used easily
— Biofuels and even some biofuel blends meet these goals.

BIOFUELS PRESENT SOLUTIONS NOW

Biofuels can be made from any type of biomass, making it completely renewable. These fuels can be used in the same way as fossil fuels, including creating chemicals used in other products such as plastics.[33] Biofuels that are used currently or being explored include:[34]
— Biomass—especially waste from manufacturing or gas created in landfills—may be used to generate power.
— E-diesel, a blend of ethanol, diesel, and additives to maintain the blend
— Ethanol
— Biodiesel
— Ethanol and biodiesel are the two most popular biofuels—especially for use in vehicles.

Did You Know? Despite the enormous potential for a range of biomass fuels to solve energy needs, the U.S. Department of Energy has chosen to prioritize its research efforts on ethanol only.[35]

ETHANOL: ETHYL OR GRAIN ALCOHOL

Ethanol is currently the most widely used biofuel, with production in the U.S. reaching some 3 to 4 billion gallons in 2004.[36,37] And manufacturing capacity is growing rapidly. Ethanol is a viable alternative fuel because it:[38]
— Doesn't contribute to global warming
— Can be blended (up to 10 percent) with gasoline
— Comes from renewable sources like corn
— Serves as an alternative for the fuel additive MTBE (methyl tertiary butyl ether), which is being phased out in many U.S. states

Yet ethanol use has resulted in an overreliance on corn to make the fuel. Even though a record 93 million acres of corn were planted in the U.S. in 2007,[39] corn prices have increased, making things difficult both for farmers and for people who rely on corn for a large part of their diet. And until farmers switch to more organic methods of fertilizing fields, corn will require high levels of natural gas–derived fertilizers to produce efficient yields.[40] Problems with deriving ethanol from corn may resolve as researchers are identifying other sources for ethanol, such as wood chips, switchgrass, and other plants.[41] In fact, ethanol can be made from any source that contains a high level of plant fiber (cellulose) or sugar.[42] Another disadvantage of ethanol is that to use it "straight" (unblended) in vehicle engines would require a "flex" fuel system that can switch between ethanol and gasoline as needed.[43]

Did You Know? An up-and-coming source of ethanol, switch-grass, grows almost everywhere in the U.S. except the far West. This native grass thrives in most conditions, requiring few pesticides or fertilizers.[44]

BIODIESEL: THE KING OF ALTERNATIVE FUELS

Have you ever developed an unexplainable yearning for French fries while driving down the road? If so, perhaps you were cruising on I-35 in Texas behind a truck driver who just filled up on Willie Nelson's Biodiesel at Carl's Corner Truck Stop. Or maybe you caught the whiff of fries in Colorado, following the fumes of a 1983 Chevy El Camino driven by the actress and sustainable living advocate Daryl Hannah or one of her colleagues. She's consulting with Grassolean LLC, a group in Telluride that began as a biodiesel-making co-op and now has its sights set on developing a nationwide chain of sustainable, green service stations. Nelson and Hannah, along with thousands of other folks who aren't as famous, are using biodiesel in their vehicles every day. While it's Willie Nelson's latest concert tour in his biodiesel-powered bus that grabs the headlines, hundreds of happy "ordinary" customers have paid Los Angeles–based Lovecraft Biofuels to retrofit their cars to run on straight veggie oil. Biodiesel is quickly making its way from celebrity gimmick to a "real-life" alternative for people like you and me.

Biodiesel, or "fatty-acid methyl ester" (as it's known in the scientific community), is derived from plant or animal oil or fat. While some people run "straight" vegetable oil in their vehicles (hence, the French fries odor), most biodiesel is created by a reaction between three types of ingredients: a form of oil, a type of alcohol, and a chemical catalyst. Vegetable or animal oil serves as the oil component. Methanol or ethanol is used as the alcohol. Lye or potassium hydrochloride is used as a catalyst. After processing, the result is 100 percent biodiesel. Biodiesel can also be mixed with petrodiesel in varying combinations.

WHY IS BIODIESEL SO GREAT?

If you're reading this book, you probably already know that biodiesel is a terrific alternative to petroleum-based diesel. But sometimes it's nice to be reminded why, so here are some of the benefits biodiesel can provide.

Most diesel vehicles need little or no modification. In most cases, 100 percent biodiesel (also called "neat" biodiesel) works well in diesel engines without modifications and has been used in automobiles, trucks, tractors and other farm equipment, commercial diesel equipment, and marine vessels.[45]

Did You Know? Biodiesel is the only current biofuel that can be used "as is" in existing vehicles.[46]

Fewer emissions. Biodiesel burns cleaner than petrodiesel, with lower levels of carbon dioxide, hydrocarbons, carbon monoxide, and particulates. It contains no sulfur, so it generates no sulfur dioxide—the substance that's implicated in acid rain. Even when mixed with petrodiesel, biodiesel substantially lowers emissions.

Doesn't contribute to global warming. Global warming is caused primarily by increased carbon dioxide emissions; biodiesel emits only the CO2 it originally contained as a plant.[47]

Naturally oxygenated. You need plenty of oxygen to achieve a good fuel "burn"—and biodiesel contains about 10 percent oxygen.

Lubricates engines. The characteristics of biodiesel cause it to provide great lubrication of engine parts. This extends engine life even beyond what would occur when using petrodiesel.

Matches petrodiesel for power and mpg. Biodiesel achieves similar power and miles-per-gallon ratings as petrodiesel.

Solving a Waste Management Crisis at Yellowstone

Xanterra Parks and Resorts runs the hotels and restaurants at many top-flight U.S. National Parks such as Yellowstone, Mount Rushmore, and the Grand Canyon.[58] Not content to simply sit back and enjoy its achievements, Xanterra decided to align its goals with those of the national parks that have brought the company such success. It decided to "go green," purchased a processor from the author's company, and began converting most of its cooking grease—more than 11,000 gallons per year—into biodiesel. Xanterra then used the biodiesel as fuel for its fleet vehicles and boilers, offsetting the purchase of some 11,000 gallons of environmental polluting petroleum diesel. Besides the environmental and economic savings from making its own biodiesel, the company even makes extra profits by selling glycerin, a byproduct of grease recycling, to a vendor for use in making facial products. So Xanterra's bottom line, not to mention its company image, is improved simply by being environmentally friendly.

According to the U.S. Department of Energy's Energy Information Administration (EIA), biodiesel has about the same energy efficiency as petrodiesel. That agency defines "energy efficiency" as "the percentage of the fuel's thermal energy that is delivered as engine output."[48] However, the "energy content" of biodiesel is about 11 percent lower than petrodiesel. This means you'll get about 11 percent lower miles-per-gallon volumetric fuel efficiency, though most users report no difference in actual fuel economy. A B20 mix (that is, 20 percent biodiesel and 80 percent petrodiesel) would result in about 2 percent fewer miles per gallon than petrodiesel.

Biodegrades. Biodiesel is biodegradable. If it spills, it will degrade naturally without harming the environment. This makes it a potentially valuable fuel for marine use. Spills in water simply break up, without damaging water or wildlife.

Is considered safe. Biodiesel is considered nontoxic, as it contains no substances that are harmful to people or the environment. Because it has a high flash point, it is unlikely to explode. Biodiesel is considered safe to handle and store. It requires nothing more than to pour it into the tank with petrodiesel when mixing. Biodiesel puts off no offensive or dangerous odors. The most potentially toxic aspect of biodiesel is during the manufacturing process, since the caustic substance lye is often used as a catalyst. By following the instructions in this book and always using safe practices, you should be able to avoid any problems with lye.

Saves you money. It is less expensive to make biodiesel than to purchase diesel. Even commercial biodiesel may be less expensive if you take advantage of any available state and federal renewable-fuel incentives. For example, large-scale biodiesel manufacturers can win U.S. Department of Agriculture grants that support increased production of biodiesel. Federal law also provides for credits on the federal fuel excise tax for use of biodiesel, as well as even biodiesel/petrodiesel blends. But if you don't want to bother with all the red tape, how much does it cost you to buy biodiesel at the pump? About $3.39 or so a gallon in August 2007, according to Pacific Biofuels' Will Noel. This compares to about $2.98 per gallon for petrodiesel in California during the same time period.[49] B20 is likely to cost you a little more or a little less than petrodiesel, depending on the distributor.[50] By contrast, many do-it-yourselfers claim that they make biodiesel at home for about $0.80 per gallon.[51] The amount you spend on setting up a biodiesel-making system can range from a few hundred to a few thousand dollars. So, the cost you pay per gallon will vary, depending on the equipment you use, the cost of your supplies, and factors such as how far you have to drive to find your source of oil.

Works in a diesel engine with no engine modifications. For more recent vehicles, there is probably no need to change anything in order to make a switch to biodiesel. If an engine has seen heavy use over the years, though, keep an eye on things as you switch to biodiesel. It is such a great lubricant that it can dislodge substances built up inside engines, causing parts to clog. Older vehicles (usually pre-1993) using rubber seals and hoses may also need monitoring, as biodiesel can cause the rubber to deteriorate.

Has broad economic and social benefits. Biodiesel contributes to energy dependence for you and your family, as well as for your country. Using vegetable and animal oils and fats supports the efforts of farmers and helps further the goal of renewability and sustainability.

Biodiesel byproducts have potential benefits. Glycerine is the byproduct of making biodiesel and is used to make soap and cosmetics. It is also being studied as an additive to livestock and poultry feed, as a replacement for antifreeze, and for dozens of other commercial uses. If you make biodiesel at home, glycerine provides a useful addition to your compost pile, and can be used to help power methane digesters to produce electricity. You may also be able to make money with it as an environmentally friendly dust-control treatment for dirt roads, driveways, and arenas It has many more uses, which this book will explain.

THE MANY USES OF BIODIESEL

If you're interested in biodiesel, you're probably thinking of pouring it into the tank of your car or truck. You may be glad to learn that biodiesel uses abound in more untraditional settings and vehicles, as well. In the sidebar below, you can read about the Arctic Cat diesel ATV that can run on biodiesel. The National Biodiesel Board has identified other uses of biodiesel:[52]

— Heating oil using a B5 blend
— Commercial lawn-care equipment
— Generators, both for home use and as diesel backup for large electrical generators
— Marine vessels, such as barges and towboats

Common sources for the oil used to make diesel include soybean oil and used restaurant oil in the U.S. and rapeseed (canola) oil in Europe.[53]

Arctic Cat to BioCat: The First Diesel ATV Uses Biodiesel

For the Arctic Cat company, using biodiesel wasn't actually at the top of the list when developing its new diesel all-terrain vehicle. The company was initially addressing sales in Europe, where diesels have always been more popular. But the Agricultural Utilization Research Institute (AURI) and the Minnesota Soybean Research and Promotion Council pitched the idea of using B20 (20 percent biodiesel and 80 percent petrodiesel)—and Arctic Cat bit. According to both Ole Tweet, vice president of new product development, and the AURI,[54] the advantages were great: B20 burns cleaner, is biodegradable, and contributes to energy independence, helping Arctic Cat meet its environmental stewardship goals. Even better, using biodiesel supports the efforts of farmers, one of Arctic Cat's most loyal customer groups.

WHY USE OR MAKE YOUR OWN BIODIESEL?

It's clear that petroleum has led us to environmental, economic, social, and political problems that are increasingly unacceptable.

Alternative fuels such as biodiesel may form part of the solution to our dependence on oil. But can one person's actions—*yours*—truly make a difference in such a dismal scenario? Remember the old "green" adage "Think globally, act locally." Short, cute, and still true. Using biodiesel—especially making your own—takes you one step closer to making your corner of the world safer and more sustainable. By using and making your own biodiesel you will support your local farmer and economy, help end the country's dependence on imported fuels (especially fossil fuels), save money, and help heal the environment. Not bad for something that McDonald's uses to fry its Chicken McNuggets in and pays to have hauled away and dumped.

BIODIESEL'S POPULARITY CONTINUES TO GROW

Maybe it's time for you to make the switch to biodiesel. It's quickly becoming the favorite alternative fuel, for many of the reasons previously discussed. Large-scale biodiesel manufacturing is growing rapidly, with a capacity of an estimated 900 million gallons in 2007, and with almost twice as much (1.7 billion gallons) capacity under construction.[55] Central Bi-Products, in Redwood Falls, Minnesota, is one biodiesel company making the fuel in a big way. They produce about 3 million gallons per year. Pacific Biodiesel is another large manufacturer of biodiesel, getting its start when an engineer was trying to help solve a waste management problem for a landfill in Hawaii.[56] Grassolean and other biodiesel co-ops are thriving throughout the U.S. And do-it-yourself biodiesel sites are springing up all around the Internet.

Does biodiesel sound like an alternative you're ready to consider? If so, you can make a switch to biodiesel easily. First off, you can purchase biodiesel or biodiesel blends commercially to use in your diesel vehicles. Even better, you can make your own biodiesel at home. This "homebrew" is every bit as potent as commercially prepared biodiesel—and can be much less expensive, especially if you join forces with friends, family, or neighbors to form a biodiesel-making co-op. The chapters in this book give you step-by-step, easy to understand instructions for how to do it yourself. Either approach you take—purchasing or making biodiesel—will benefit both your pocketbook *and* the world around you.

ALL ABOUT BIODIESEL

By now, you've been hearing about biodiesel from your friends or family or colleagues at work, or maybe from television, newspapers, or the Internet. Everywhere you turn there's another story about it. Biodiesel is in a significant growth stage right now, because of various factors: the rising cost of petroleum-based fuels, the emissions from such fuels, the realization that our oil reserves won't last forever, and so on. Most states are beginning to mandate that all diesel fuel sold at the pumps must contain a blend of biodiesel.

The National Biodiesel Board (NBB) has provided some estimates of sales volume in the United States.[59]

The use and manufacturing of biodiesel is growing exponentially, as shown on the chart below. Local governments, transit agencies, trucking companies, and even the military—all are moving toward the use of biodiesel in their fleets.

State legislation involving biodiesel is at an all-time high. The NBB has tracked more than 275 pieces of biodiesel-specific legislation in the 2006 state sessions. A total of 53 bills passed,

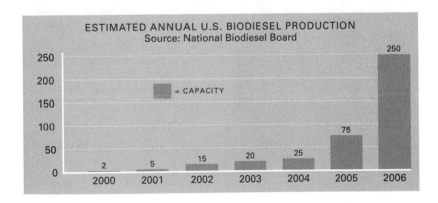

directly affecting biodiesel use and production. Some of these may be significant to you in your own state or region.

HISTORY OF BIODIESEL

Let's pause for a moment and take a look at the origins of biodiesel and how it works in a diesel engine. Dr. Rudolf Diesel, a son of Bavarian immigrants to France who became a machinist, a designer, and a noted refrigerator engineer, invented the first "Diesel" engine in 1892. He designed it to run on a number of fuels, including vegetable oil. He commented that it would help considerably in the development of agriculture of the countries that used his engine. He demonstrated his engine at the World Exhibition in Paris in 1900 and described an experiment using peanut oil as fuel in his engine. (Although straight peanut oil isn't considered true biodiesel, it and other vegetable oils are the base for most biodiesel.)

While biodiesel has actually been around for about 100 years, the cheap availability of petroleum made it and other fossil fuels the fuel of choice for diesel engines. But now that petrodiesel prices have risen so high, it's finally becoming affordable to use biodiesel. Due in part to the government's EPAct policy of 1992, biodiesel

is finally becoming a mainstream fuel of choice. In fact, it's becoming highly popular in many countries around the world. People in a number of nations are paying upward of $4 a gallon for petrodiesel. For those countries, biodiesel could be a highly beneficial alternative fuel, in terms of the cost savings alone.

THE VERY FIRST DIESEL MOTOR

State Legislation in 2006 Session Dealing with Biodiesel

Among the proposals announced or enacted in this year's sessions:

Arizona Gov. Janet Napolitano signed an executive order in September committing the state to reduce carbon dioxide and other greenhouse gas emissions and creating a state panel to develop a plan to achieve the goal. The advisory group's recommendations include increasing the use of renewable energy sources; improving energy efficiency; using low-emissions state vehicles; adopting cleaner-emission standards for vehicles and increasing production of ethanol and biodiesel.

California Gov. Arnold Schwarzenegger issued an Executive Order that, among other things, establishes a target for the state of California to produce and use a minimum of 20 percent of its biofuels within California by 2010, 40 percent by 2020 and 75 percent by 2050. That includes both ethanol and biodiesel.

Florida Gov. Jeb Bush signed the Florida Energy Act, which provides for sales tax exemptions and investment tax credits for costs associated with renewable energy technologies, which includes biodiesel.

Illinois Gov. Rod R. Blagojevich unveiled a new plan in August that would replace 50 percent of the state's current supply of imported oil with renewable homegrown biofuels like ethanol and biodiesel. The plan would also invest $25 million to help build five new biodiesel plants. Additionally, the plan would provide new incentives to drive continued investment in the state's biofuels industry, and increase public availability.

Indiana Gov. Mitch Daniels signed an extension of a law that increases the maximum amount of credits that may be granted for biodiesel production, biodiesel blending, and ethanol production. It also extends a tax credit for the retail sale of blended biodiesel to 2010.

Iowa Gov. Tom Vilsack in May signed into law two renewable fuels and infrastructure bills that provide point-of-sale retailers with a three cent income tax credit on each gallon of a two percent (B2) blend or higher. The legislation also establishes a renewable fuels standard requiring that 25 percent of a retailer's fuel sales be ethanol or biodiesel by 2020.

Michigan Gov. Jennifer Granholm announced in August that the state is setting aside $250,000 to help service station owners convert gasoline pumps to alternative fuel pumps. The hope is that the grants will lead to 1,000 alternative fuel pumps installed or converted by 2008—a 20 percent increase. This is the second round of grants being made available by the state.

New York Gov. George Pataki signed several pieces of legislation related to biodiesel, including a biofuel production tax credit of 15 cents per gallon after the first 40,000 gallons produced; elimination of all motor fuel taxes on alternative fuels; cost-share infrastructure grants for private sector gas stations to install and/or convert pumps for B20 or E85; and a residential Bioheat® fuel tax credit in residential heating applications.

Pennsylvania Gov. Edward G. Rendell launched a new plan in May—"PennSecurity Fuels Initiative"—to reduce the nation's dependence on foreign oil by replacing 900 million gallons of the state's transportation fuels over the next decade with alternative sources, such as ethanol and biodiesel. It also requires that a certain percentage of retail transportation fuel sales contain eligible fuels such as biodiesel. It invests in infrastructure to support the increased use of alternative fuels and provides incentives that open new markets to Pennsylvania farmers who grow the feedstock to produce biofuels.

Source: National Biodiesel Board website, *www.nbb.org.* [Readers may wish to visit this site for updates on state legislation and other developments.]

BIODIESEL DEFINED

In simple terms, biodiesel is a domestically produced, renewable fuel that can be manufactured from vegetable oils, animal fats, or recycled restaurant greases. Homemade biodiesel is usually made from used restaurant oil, since most people can get that for free in a kind of beneficial "aftermarket." It can also be made from semiclean to very nasty, rancid-looking cooking oils, tallow, or animal fats (though homebrew biodiesel makers are advised to stick with the better oils).

Biodiesel is safe, it's biodegradable, and it reduces serious air pollutants such as particulates, carbon monoxide, hydrocarbons, and air toxins. It has many other benefits we'll list later.

The end result of the biodiesel-making process is a high-quality fuel that *acts just like petrodiesel* to any diesel engine, *with no modifications needed.* That's an oversimplification of the process, but it gives you an idea of what's involved.

Technically speaking, biodiesel is defined as the mono-alkyl esters of fatty acids derived from vegetable oils or animal fats. It's known chemically as a "methyl ester." In simpler terms, biodiesel is the end product of a vegetable oil or animal fat that has been chemically reacted with an alcohol and a catalyst to remove the glycerine; the chemical produced is known as a fatty-acid methyl ester, or biodiesel. To achieve this reaction, a strong "catalyst" such as sodium hydroxide (lye) or potassium hydroxide (KOH) must be added to the alcohol.

Biodiesel can be made from methanol or from ethanol (derived from crops such as corn). Other "higher" alcohols such as isopropanol and butanol have also been used, but there are numerous problems with using them. Using alcohols of higher molecular weights improves the cold flow properties of the resulting ester, at the cost of a less efficient transesterification reaction. When made from methanol the ester is called methyl ester, and when made from ethanol it's called ethyl ester.

Because of the large price difference between ethanol and methanol, biodiesel is usually made from the latter, which in turn is most commonly made from natural gas but can also be made from renewable resources such as municipal solid waste and biomass crops. Of course, this would be a preferred method of producing methanol, as it then would be considered a renewable alcohol. Since ethanol is already a renewable resource, it may become the alcohol of choice for making biodiesel if the price drops enough to become economically feasible.

HOW BIODIESEL IS MADE

The high-quality diesel fuel known as biodiesel is made through a chemical process called *transesterification*. Don't let the big word scare you, because the process is relatively simple to perform—when you're given the proper guidance, equipment, and experience (about which this book will inform you). Transesterification is essentially the process of breaking down the oil molecule to replace one form of alcohol (glycerine) with another (methanol).

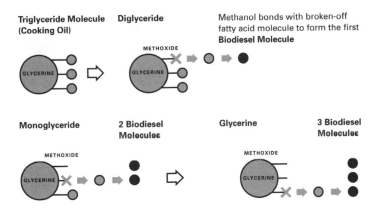

GLYCERINE SETTLED OUT OF BIODIESEL

If you educate yourself thoroughly about biodiesel, you can make high-quality biodiesel at home. You should take note that not all used oil will work in a homebrew application, but more on that later. The only major ingredients you'll need are used cooking oil (free, from restaurants), methanol, and either lye (NaOH) or potassium hydroxide (KOH). You can also make biodiesel from new oil sources. Everything needed is readily available. In later sections I'll tell you where to find these resources and exactly what to look for in your oil sources.

The chemical reaction that occurs through this process breaks down the cooking oil into a layer of biodiesel that rises to the top of the reactor, and a layer of glycerine that falls to the bottom. The glycerine byproduct is drained off and used for other purposes, which I'll also cover later. The biodiesel is then washed, dried, and filtered to remove any extra impurities. It's then ready to be used as a fuel in diesel engines *without any modifications* to the engine. Because biodiesel is only a little more viscous than diesel, it will flow with ease through a diesel fuel system. It can readily be mixed with petrodiesel simply by adding it to your fuel tank. No actual stirring or anything else is required, so if you are traveling, you can add petrodiesel at any time, in any proportion.

When making your own biodiesel, most of the time you'll get fairly close to a 90 to 100 percent yield of biodiesel out of your used oil. It will probably be less than 100 percent, but basically if you put in 20 gallons of used oil, you'll get back roughly 18 to 20 gallons of biodiesel.

Biodiesel blends are stated in terms such as "B20" or "B100." These are easy to decipher: Just read the number after the "B" as the percentage of biodiesel versus petrodiesel. For example, B100 is pure biodiesel (100 percent), while B20 is a blend of 20 percent biodiesel and 80 percent petrodiesel. B100 is also referred to as "neat" fuel (just as ordering a "neat whiskey" at a bar yields you a drink with no mixer).

THE EPACT AND BIODIESEL

Luckily for its growing popularity, biodiesel is considered an official alternative fuel under the Energy Policy Act of 1992 (commonly called the "EPAct"), which Congress passed to attempt to reduce our nation's dependence on imported petroleum. Among other things, the act requires certain vehicle fleets to acquire vehicles running on alternative fuel, meaning fuel not made with petroleum (a fossil fuel, and nonreplenishable). The U.S. Department of Energy administers the regulations through the following:
— Federal fleet requirements
— State and alternative fuel provider rule
— Private and local government fleet rule
— Alternative Fuel Designation Authority

Fleets looking to comply with the EPAct must use fuel blends that contain at least 20 percent biodiesel.[60]

INTENT OF THE EPACT

The goal of the EPAct is to enhance the nation's energy security. Several parts of the act were designed to encourage the use of alternative fuels, to help reduce U.S. dependence on imported oil. EPAct requirements apply to certain fleets of 20 or more vehicles that meet specific requirements.

In January 2007, President George W. Bush signed Executive Order (E.O.) 13423: "Strengthening Federal Environmental, Energy, and Transportation Management," a mandate that requires agencies with 20 or more vehicles in the United States to decrease petroleum consumption by 2 percent per year relative to their fiscal year (FY)

DO IT YOURSELF GUIDE TO BIODIESEL

Easy Biodiesel Process Flowchart
Shows the general process flow for making biodiesel with our processors.
This is a simplified chart showing an overview of the whole process.

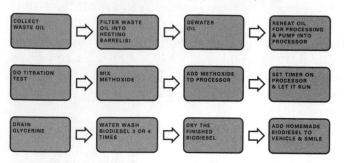

The entire process takes about 2½ days.
Actual hands-on time is only about 1½ hours.

2005 baseline through FY 2015. The order also requires agencies to increase alternative fuel use by 10 percent per year relative to the previous year. E.O. 13423 revokes an earlier executive order, 13149, which was signed in April 2000.

Biodiesel is one of the accepted fuels under the EPAct program. The biodiesel used can be either B100 or B20. B20 users must use more total fuel, but they still get credit under the act. If you think your business might qualify, read more about it.[61]

EPACT ALTERNATIVE FUELS LIST

— Methanol, ethanol, and other alcohols
— Blends of 85 percent or more of alcohol with gasoline
— Natural gas and liquid fuels domestically produced from natural gas
— Liquefied petroleum gas (propane)
— Coal-derived liquid fuels
— Hydrogen
— Electricity
— Biodiesel (B100)*
— Fuels (other than alcohol) derived from biological materials

For more information about alternative fuels on the Department of Energy website, please visit the Alternative Fuels Data Center at *www.eere.energy.gov/afdc/altfuel/altfuels.html.*

* In January 2001, the biodiesel Final Rule made it possible for fleets to earn EPAct credits for use of biodiesel blends of at least 20 percent. This rule does not make B20 (a blend of 20 percent biodiesel with 80 percent diesel) an alternative fuel, but it gives one credit for every 450 gallons of pure biodiesel used in biodiesel blends.

WHAT CAN BIODIESEL BE MADE FROM?

Biodiesel can be made from many oil feedstock plants. Soybeans are *currently* the most commonly used feedstock, though many other plants have great potential as a biodiesel feedstock. While hundreds of plants can be used to produce the oil for making biodiesel, the ones that seem to have the most potential are jatropha, canola (or rapeseed), sunflower seeds, palm oil, and algae. Even the sometimes controversial hemp seed can produce biodiesel (interestingly, the fuel is quite green in color). Currently, soybeans account for approximately 90 percent of the feedstock supply for biodiesel. This is primarily due to the current availability of soy as a feedstock. It is likely, though, that another feedstock will eventually replace soy, because several others have higher yields as well as other desirable characteristics for biodiesel.

Commercially, vegetable oils are evaluated for use as a biofuel, rated on criteria such as:

— Suitability as a fuel, based on flash point, energy content, viscosity, combustion products, and other factors
— Cost, based in part on yield, effort required to grow and harvest, and postharvest processing cost

EXAMPLES OF FEEDSTOCKS USED TO MAKE BIODIESEL

— Cold-weather performance; some oils will produce biodiesel that gels at temperatures as high as 65°F, while others will be suitable for below 40°F

For the person making biodiesel at home, the main considerations are cost, quality, and (in certain regions of the country) cold-weather performance.

One of the most talked-about feedstocks in biodiesel newsgroups and forums is **algae**. Microalgae have much faster growth rates than terrestrial crops. The yield of oil from algae is estimated to be from between 5,000 to 20,000 gallons per acre per year. This is 7 to 30 times greater than the next best crop, Chinese tallow (or 699 gallons per acre per year). This gives algae huge potential as a biodiesel feedstock, so right now there's a lot of buzz about algae.

In addition, algae can be use to clean up CO_2 emissions from places like coal-fired power plants that produce huge amounts of CO_2 (which contributes to greenhouse warming). It turns out that algae consume the CO_2 and produce oxygen in its place. So this makes it a win–win feedstock, on multiple levels.

Algal-oil processes into biodiesel as easily as oil derived from land-based crops. The difficulties in efficient biodiesel production from algae lie more in finding the ideal strain of algae, developing an efficient cultivation and harvesting method, and determining where and how to grow it.

Another oil with great promise is the jatropha plant. **Jatropha oil** is vegetable oil produced from the seeds of the *Jatropha curcas*, a plant that can grow in wastelands. The *Jatropha plant* grows almost anywhere, even on poor sandy soils, gravelly soil, or other soils that most plants wouldn't survive in. It can thrive on these soils and grow even in rock crevices. After the oil is extracted from the plant, the remaining biomass can be used to power electricity plants. One reason I mention this oil is the plant's high yield: It produces more than four times as much oil as soybeans, and more than 10 times that of corn. A hectare (2.47 acres) of jatropha produces over 490 gallons of oil, while soy produces only about 118 gallons of oil.

JATROPHA

YIELDS OF COMMON CROPS (U.S. GALLONS PER ACRE)	
Corn	18
Hemp	39
Soybean	48
Camelina	62
Sunflowers	102
Peanuts	113
Rapeseed (canola)	127
Jatropha	202
Palm oil	635
Chinese tallow	699
Algae	5,000

See the Resources section for more information about crop yields.

It's not just new oil that can be used, however. Makers of biodiesel can also process used vegetable oil from restaurants, kitchens, potato chip companies, and the like, essentially recycling this waste oil. It is estimated that every year approximately 4.5 *billion* gallons of used vegetable oil are available in the United States alone. This could potentially become a lot of clean-burning, renewable biodiesel.

Commercial biodiesel is mostly made from virgin oils, which is great for our country's economy, as these oils can be grown by our own farmers. By making or using biodiesel, you're not only helping yourself, you're also doing something good for the environment, while helping support farmers in our country.

SVO VS. BIODIESEL

Maybe you've heard about people running SVO in their diesel engine, and wondered what SVO is and how it differs from biodiesel.

SVO stands for "straight vegetable oil." SVO users run straight vegetable oil in their engines. To use SVO in a diesel requires fairly extensive and expensive modifications to a vehicle, because of the oil's high viscosity. Modifications usually include two fuel tanks: one, a heated tank for SVO; the other, a tank for regular petrodiesel. To use SVO requires starting the vehicle on petrodiesel, then switching over to SVO once the oil is heated up to the required temperature. Heating the oil is required to reduce the viscosity to a usable level. To shut down requires switching back to petrodiesel for a time; this prevents the thick oil from remaining in the lines when the engine is shut off. If you forget to switch back, you run the risk of the SVO getting thick and your not being able to start the engine again.

SVO systems often require expensive prefilters to clean up the waste oil, plus they need heated fuel filters, lines, switches, and much more. Also, many vehicles are not at all suited to run on SVO, due to fuel pump design and fuel injectors. SVO users typically change filters every 200 to 300 miles due to clogging, which is not only expensive but time consuming. While SVO burns well in many older diesels, it doesn't start the engine, and may "coke" in the injectors as a hot engine cools.

Biodiesel, by contrast, doesn't require thinning in the tank (the transesterification process does that), and it requires *no modifications whatsoever* to your engine. The only drawback is the initial processor purchase. The advantages are that you get to keep the processor forever, you're making an EPA-approved fuel, and you'll recoup your costs usually in about six months. In addition, you can share the expense of the system with family or friends and recoup the costs even faster. After that, you get to drive for about one-third the cost, or less, of what everyone else is paying.

Biodiesel is approved by virtually all the major vehicle and heavy equipment manufacturers.

With an SVO system, however, you have a large upfront expense and continual filter expenses, and must make extensive modifications to your engine (which will void your warranty). If you sell your SVO-equipped vehicle, you lose the system and have to start over. Beyond that, SVO is *not* an EPA-approved fuel and is *not* approved by any major vehicle and engine manufacturer. When burning SVO, you still have the glycerine in the oil, which is nearly impossible to burn. This results in "coking" and deposits that, over time, can cause you a lot of problems. With an older diesel you might pull it off with minimal problems, but you'll have to decide whether it's worth the risk and the expense.

COMMON VEHICLE FOR SVO USE

Commercial biodiesel does have standards that must be met, just like commercial petrodiesel does. The ASTM Standard for Biodiesel is ASTM D6751. (ASTM International is an international standards-developing organization that develops and publishes voluntary technical standards for a wide range of materials, products, systems, and services.) When made to this standard, biodiesel is a very-high-quality fuel that is superior to petrodiesel in every way *except* in cold-weather performance.

With the rapidly rising demand for biodiesel and alternative fuels, a lot of people are working hard to improve the cold-weather performance of biodiesel to equal that of petrodiesel. That difference should disappear sometime in the near future. To avoid problems with your fuel, however, you should try to make the highest quality fuel possible.

If you follow the important points in this book, you'll be able to produce a high-quality biodiesel fuel that fully meets ASTM standards.

It's important to understand the entire process if you intend to build your own processor. If you buy a processor from a reputable company, and you follow its guidelines closely, you should achieve the goal of producing high-quality fuel.

An ASTM 6751 Test Includes:

ASTM D445: Viscosity at 40°C

ASTM D664: Acid number

ASTM D6584: Free and total glycerine

ASTM D1160: Distillation temperature

ASTM D613: Cetane number

ASTM D2500: Cloud point

ASTM D93: Flash point, Pensky Martens

ASTM D5453: Sulfur

ASTM D4951: Phosphorus, sodium, potassium, calcium, and magnesium

ASTM D2709: Sediment and water

ASTM D874: Sulfated ash

ASTM D4530: Carbon residue

ASTM D130: Copper strip corrosion rating

BENEFITS OF BIODIESEL

Maybe you're wondering whether biodiesel is as good in your tank as petrodiesel. The answer is, it's better, in almost every aspect.

— It's made from **renewable** resources, such as soybean, sunflower, canola, and other plants.

— It **reduces our dependence** on oil from foreign countries and contributes to our own society.

— It **requires no wars** and lost lives, the way petrodiesel does.

— It **burns up to 90 percent cleaner** than conventional diesel fuel made from fossil fuels. It substantially reduces unburned hydrocarbons, carbon monoxide, and particulate matter in exhaust fumes. It eliminates sulfur dioxide emissions. *Biodiesel contains no sulfur*, so is even cleaner than the new ULSD (ultra low-sulfur diesel).

— It's considered an **alternative fuel** under the EPAct.

— It's **plant-based** and considered carbon neutral, because it adds almost no CO2 to the atmosphere, since the plants that it's made from consume CO2 and produce oxygen.

— Its potential for forming ozone emissions is nearly half that of conventional diesel fuel.

— It's **pleasant smelling,** both in its raw form and when burned.

— It's **safe**. It's considered nontoxic and greatly reduces the amount of cancer-causing emissions, compared to petrodiesel.

— It has a **flash point twice as high** as petrodiesel, making it much less likely to ignite in a car wreck or spill in your shop.

— It's less toxic than table salt and biodegrades as fast as sugar.

— It can be used straight in warmer weather (as B100) or can be blended with petrodiesel in any ratio and splash mixes with no mechanical mixers needed.

— It requires no engine modifications to use.

— It **has increased lubricity.** Biodiesel has *greatly* increased lubricating properties versus petrodiesel, even in very small blends of as little as 2 percent bio. With today's ULSD, which is a very dry fuel, adding as little as 2 percent biodiesel can give back the lubricity that the ULSD takes away.

— It can reduce the classic diesel engine "knocking" noise.

— It has a higher cetane rating

— It **produces savings for your budget.** Biodiesel made at home can be made for about 75 cents a gallon.

Today's diesels are sophisticated engines capable of amazing power. If you're already the owner of a diesel vehicle, I'm sure you don't want to sacrifice power just to burn biodiesel. Well, you don't have to. Biodiesel is basically capable of making as much power as petrodiesel. It actually has a little less BTU power, but because of several factors (such as the fact that it's much better at lubricating and has a higher cetane rating), you end up with about the same power. Most people feel they have more power, though results will vary.

Skeptical about power? Check out images of the world's first diesel dragster running a ¼ mile dragstrip in 7.98 seconds and achieving speeds of 167 mph with a Cummins diesel engine and biodiesel.[62]

BIODIESEL-POWERED DRAGSTER (PHOTO COURTESY CUMMINSRACING.COM)

FUEL LUBRICATION

These days, the federal government has mandated the use of ULSD, in an attempt to reduce the sulfur emissions in most diesel fuel sold at the pump. The move to lower sulfur content is expected to allow the application of newer emissions control technologies that should substantially lower emissions of noxious particulates from diesel engines, similar to changes that previously took place in the European Union.

Ultra-low sulfur diesel was proposed by the Environmental Protection Agency as a new standard for the sulfur content in on-road diesel fuel sold in the U.S. since October 15, 2006, except for California and parts of Alaska. California required it since September 1, 2006, and rural Alaska will transition all diesel to ULSD in 2010. This new regulation applies to all diesel fuel, diesel fuel additives, and distillate fuels blended with diesel for on-road use, such as kerosene, though it doesn't yet apply to train locomotives, marine, or off-road uses. By December 1, 2010, all highway diesel will be ULSD. Farmers running off-road diesel will see low-sulfur diesel mandated for No. 2 diesel in 2007, and ULSD in 2010 that requires the use of additives or biodiesel to regain the lost lubricity.

ULSD contains even fewer lubricants, because removing the sulfur also removes most of the lubricants. By adding as little as 2 percent biodiesel to the blend, you get the lubricating properties back. With higher concentrations

ULTRA LOW-SULFUR DIESEL FUEL
(15-PPM Sulfur Maximum)
Required for use in all model year 2007 and later highway diesel vehicles and engines. Recommended for use in all diesel vehicles and engines.

you could achieve even better lubricating qualities. And because biodiesel lubricates moving parts better, your engine should last longer and run quieter too.

SAVINGS EXAMPLES

Here's an example of what you can save. In my example I'll assume you drive only 20,000 miles a year, you average 14 mpg in your diesel truck, and you pay fuel prices of $3.10 per gallon of regular diesel. So let's say you use 1,428 gallons of fuel costing $4,428. If you burned B100 at $0.76 cents a gallon, you'd spend $1,085 and would save $3,343 per year. Think about that! That's a lot of money saved in one year for just one vehicle. If you have two diesel vehicles in your family, or drive more than 20,000 miles in a year, the savings are much higher. Many of us drive far more miles than that every year, so these are conservative estimates.

If you figure the savings monthly, that's about $279 per month. With the money you save, you could nearly make a payment on a new diesel vehicle to buy your biodiesel in.

TIP: Try using an easy-to-use interactive savings calculator that allows you to input your mileage driven, price per gallon, and so on. Visit our webpage at *www.ezbiodiesel.com/bookbonus.htm* and look for the "Savings Calculator" link.

DRAWBACKS OF BIODIESEL

While biodiesel is a superior high-quality fuel, you should be aware of a few possible concerns, such as performance issues in cold climates, solvency issues in older vehicles, and fuel tank clogging and bacteria growth.

COLD WEATHER ISSUES

Because biodiesel is made from organic cooking oils and animal fats, it gels (turns semisolid) at a warmer temperature than petrodiesel. The temperature at which it starts to gel varies according to the feedstock the fuel is made from, but soy-based biodiesel will start to gel at around 32°F, and canola-based RME (rapeseed methyl ester) will start to gel at about 14°F. Other feedstocks, such as palm oil or peanut oil, may start to gel at much higher temperatures, making them suitable only for tropical climates.

For comparison, nonwinterized 100 percent diesel fuel has a cloud point of about 20°F and a gel point of about 0°F. Winterized petrodiesel can be much lower. While you should note some cold-weather drawbacks to biodiesel, there are ways around this if you live in an area that has colder climates in the winter (say, regularly below 40°F). One of the most common methods right now is to blend in petrodiesel with the biodiesel. This is usually accomplished with blends from B20 to B50. (Remember that the number after the "B" refers to the percentage of biodiesel in the blend.) Chapter 12, "Improving Your Fuel's Cold-Weather Performance," contains additional suggestions for dealing with biodiesel in cold climes.

MATERIAL COMPATIBILITY CONCERNS

Another problem with biodiesel is that it dissolves some forms of cheap plastics and natural rubber. Typically this occurs only in certain older vehicles dating to 1993 and earlier. Some people have run a lot of biodiesel through their older vehicles with few or no problems. Just be aware of this, and consider replacing your rubber fuel lines and parts with newer synthetic lines. Otherwise, if you have an older vehicle, you should inspect fuel lines regularly until you're sure that they are OK. Look for lines that are swollen, spongy, seeping, sticky, or otherwise showing signs of deterioration. If you spot any of these conditions, replace them with synthetic lines.

FUEL FILTER CLOGGING

Who knew? It turns out that biodiesel is an excellent cleaner of fuel systems. Although this property is basically good, it could also pose a problem in older vehicles if this cleansing action loosened accumulated deposits and debris, possibly clogging your fuel filter. Symptoms of this might include rough idling, stalling, hard starting, and the like. This too is easily fixed, simply by swapping in a new fuel filter. If you have an older vehicle (say, made before 1993), or one with over 100,000 miles on the odometer, I suggest that you keep a new fuel filter on hand, then drive a few hundred to a few thousand miles on biodiesel, and after that change the filter. You might have to change it again, slightly sooner than usual, after the next few thousand miles. After that, this shouldn't be a problem. Newer vehicles likely won't experience this.

FUEL TANK BACTERIA

If you already have bacterial growth in your fuel tank, there's a small chance that adding biodiesel will cause the problem to accelerate. This is rarely an issue when making biodiesel on a small scale, though, and is more often a problem with fleet users (which operate multiple vehicles). The primary reason for this is that biodiesel tends to absorb water more readily than does petrodiesel. When fleet users store the fuel in large tanks, they often inadvertently expose it to more air when they draw the fuel level down, which in turn allows more moisture to be absorbed, thus feeding the bacteria.

There's a simple solution, though. Additives, called biocides, are available to kill this bacteria. You might want to add some of this to your first tank or two of biodiesel, just to be sure. Then add some every few months or so as a precaution. If you do store fuel in large quantities, you should add a biocide more often. A biocide is relatively cheap; a $20 bottle will treat over 1,000 gallons. Purchased in greater volume, the biocide will cost even less.

For commercial users, or anyone using large amounts of biodiesel and therefore storing a large volume, an occasional biocide treatment is a completely safe, relatively inexpensive way to ward off potential problems.

Note that petrodiesel is also susceptible to fuel tank bacteria, though biodiesel has a slightly higher probability of this happening.

Proper handling and storage can reduce the opportunities for bacteria to grow in the fuel. Some ideas for proper storage include avoiding air in large tanks (air can hold moisture), storing away from direct sunlight (which causes heat, stimulating growth), eliminating water from ever getting in the tanks, storing fuel in properly cleaned and well-maintained tanks, and storing fuel for shorter periods.

BIOCIDE

The bottom line is that if you're concerned about your vehicle being compatible with biodiesel, you might want to run only B20 until you resolve your concerns. B20 has been proven to be safe in virtually every type of automobile, and is what you would buy at most commercial pumps.

CHAPTER 2

FINDING, TESTING, AND STORING USED COOKING OIL

You can acquire used cooking oil from a variety of places, some better than others. Homebrewers of biodiesel tend to agree that the best oil is usually found at Chinese food restaurants. They generally use better oil, and change it more often, though of course this varies. Some of the *worst* oil for biodiesel is found at the big fast-food restaurants. Avoid them if at all possible, because they usually overuse their oil, which raises the FFAs (free fatty acids) in the oil, making it much harder to process. Usually, the better the food at a restaurant, the better the quality of its used oil, because the chef and owner will have found that overusing the oil makes their food taste worse and drives away diners. It's a truism that restaurants that take better care of their diners by serving them better food also take better care of their oil.

When considering where to find oil for your processing, make a short checklist for yourself. Answer the following questions: How often do they change their oil? (If they go longer than once a week, be wary, though it may still be useable.) How much oil do they go through each week? What kind of pickup system do they require? (*Example:* Will they put

TYPICAL GREASE TRASH RECEPTACLE

it back in the carboys it came in, or do you need to supply 30- or 55-gallon barrels?) Do they add water to their waste oil? (Sounds strange, but one of my restaurant suppliers was dumping some wash water into the oil initially, until I found out. Once I started picking up their oil, they agreed to keep water out of the oil. That much water in your oil can ruin your biodiesel or be difficult to remove.)

Also note on your checklist how much food sludge is in the supplier's oil. This is hard to tell merely by looking at a barrel full of oil, so you might have to ask. Some restaurants will scrape so much food debris into the oil that you'll end up with about 20 to 50 percent food sludge with each pickup. The more food debris, the faster the oil goes rancid, which can smell terrible. The smell can be unbearable in the summer, but not so bad in the winter if you're storing it outdoors. Plus, you'll have to properly dispose of the sludge. You'll need to decide how much you can handle, but the less the better. You might ask the restaurant if they can pour the discarded oil through a filter into a bucket or carboy. You could even provide them a 5-gallon bucket filter to prefilter the oil before giving it to you.

IDEAS FOR WHERE TO FIND USED OIL

You can find oil for your processing in a wide variety of locations.
— Chinese restaurants are generally considered the best.
— Virtually all restaurants will have some oil available.
— Bakeries (surprisingly, one large doughnut chain I spoke with said that all its oil ends up in the doughnuts; this shocked me, but you may have better luck.)
— Retirement homes (which usually have their own kitchens)
— Hospitals
— Schools
— Large companies that may have their own in-house cafeterias or food vendors. Some go through thousands of gallons of oil each month.
— Potato chip companies (smaller companies may be more willing to work with you.)

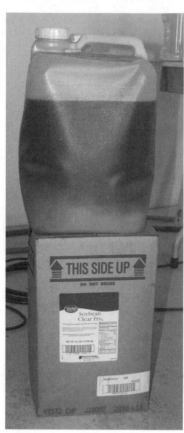

CARBOY OF USED COOKING OIL

— Special events such as fairs, concerts, and open-air festivals, which may have many vendors left with waste oil afterward and eager to get rid of it quickly. Go around the first day and offer to pick up their oil at the end of the event (and be sure to confirm your intention in writing, or at least by phone or fax, and don't leave them hanging). Or contact the event organizers to offer your services.

— Many people fry turkeys these days, so offer to pick up used oil after the holidays.

— Rendering companies (though you'll have to pay for their oil)

HOW TO GET THE OIL

Now you have some ideas for where to find used oil, and you're thinking about the best way to talk someone else into letting you pick up their used oil. You can go about this in several ways. I'll outline a few ideas here.

Probably the best idea is to scope out a likely restaurant (preferably one serving Chinese food), then simply have lunch there at around 2 p.m. (their slow time). When you're about finished eating, tell your server that you really enjoyed the meal, and ask if you may speak with the owner or manager. If you don't tell them you enjoyed the meal first, the manager is likely to come out acting defensive, thinking you have a complaint, which isn't the way you want to start things off. Then simply explain that you're making biodiesel fuel for your own car, for your personal use only (not to resell), and you'd be interested in regularly picking up their used oil. Explain clearly that you'd be reliable and clean, and you'd promise never to leave them hanging with a full barrel of oil. You must also be ready to supply them with a 55-gallon drum, if needed. Another good idea is to present them with something like a postcard, business card, or typewritten sheet with all your contact information. Be sure to give them two or three phone numbers to reach you or your colleagues, so they know you'll be easy to reach should they need a quick oil pickup.

I've found that owners seem more open to giving their used oil to me, or to my work partners or colleagues, when we assure them that we'll only be using it ourselves, and will be putting it to a good, environmentally friendly use. They like knowing that you'll use it to make biodiesel, as they too are fed up with our foreign oil dependency. Plus they won't have to pay a firm to pick up the oil, you'll be reliable and honest, and they'll be glad to save the money.

Don't try to lie to them about your use, but don't offer more information than necessary, either—as that can raise too many questions. One of my current sources is the owner of six restaurants, and in fact they make biodiesel from their used oil. But they had too much, so they agreed to let us pick up the oil from one restaurant only. They knew we wanted it because we mailed them a politely worded postcard to that effect.

Another way we've had some success has been with direct mailings. You could put together a postcard or letter that says something like this:

> *Hello, my name is Joe Smith and I would like to offer a proposal that could benefit both of us. I would like to offer to begin picking up your used cooking oil, to make biodiesel fuel for my own personal use. I am not a business, but would promise to pick up the oil on a regular basis, and to never leave you with full containers of oil. This could save you some money if you are paying to have it picked up now, and I would be able to turn it into an environmentally friendly fuel, which will also save me some money. Biodiesel also helps to reduce our dependence on foreign oil, and therefore we may not have to fight as many wars one day, if we can continue to reduce our need for foreign oil. Thank you. Joe Smith 555-1234.*

That's just an idea, which you can modify to suit your needs. Print up some of these letters, then copy your target addresses out of the phone book and mail them out. You might want to start with only 15 or 20 at a time, to avoid being overwhelmed. You might get as few as 1 or 2 responses per mailing, but they do work for us.

Another option is landfills. Some landfills may accept used cooking grease, and may let you take it off their hands. You might even try running a small ad in a newspaper or other periodical.

I suggest that you never take oil without asking. Grease dumpsters are privately owned, and if you just take it *you are stealing.* Some would argue that used oil is a waste product, or that the restaurant owner said it was OK. But that doesn't change the fact that you are taking it without permission. Once the oil is in their grease dumpster or barrel, it may no longer be the restaurant's property if they signed a contract with the collection company that states this. Even if the oil is in a barrel, it might be reserved for another biodiesel person like you who's trying to collect some oil. You wouldn't like it if someone stole your oil (we've had it happen, and had to implement timely, and expensive, theft prevention methods). So **please don't steal oil.**

IDEAS FOR COLLECTING USED OIL

You have many options for collecting the used oil. Of course, I can't tell you exactly how to do it, because it depends on whom you are getting it from, what they need, what equipment you have available, and so on. But I can give you some ideas. Be sure to check our website (*www.ezbiodiesel.com/bookbonus.com*), as we may carry some of the items you need, along with additional photos.

CARBOYS

If you will not be picking up large amounts from your supplier, you might be able to get them to pour the oil back into the original carboy (or cubee container) that it came in. (Curiously enough, "carboy" comes from the Arabic word *qarrabah,* or "big jug.") That can give you an easy way to collect it, as you just grab the carboys and load them up. Many restaurants don't want to mess with trying to pour oil back into the smaller containers.

5-GALLON BUCKETS

You could buy several 5-gallon buckets with lids and let the restaurant pour the oil into those. This might be easier for some of their staff to manage. Buckets are small enough to load into a car or pickup bed by hand, by just one person.

55-GALLON DRUMS

Now we're getting into some challenging areas. If you use a 55-gallon drum, you'll have to load or pump out a full barrel of oil. The advantage is that you can go longer between pickups, and the barrels have a handy opening to pour the oil into (provided that you supply the restaurant with an open-head drum).

There are two types of drums: open head and closed head. Open head means it has a removable lid, whereas a closed head drum does not. A closed-head drum has one or more bung openings. I really don't suggest a closed-head drum and funnel, as it makes the top of the funnel too high for some restaurant workers, plus it can be difficult and messy for them. If they are inconvenienced, they're likely to go back to the grease dumpster method. When selecting a drum, you have a choice of steel or polyethylene. Either is fine for storing biodiesel or cooking oil, but only steel is suitable for heating.

CLOSED-HEAD DRUM

OPEN-HEAD DRUM WITH LID ATTACHED (PHOTO COURTESY GRAYDON BLAIR, UTAH BIODIESEL SUPPLY)

Tip: Don't leave the locking ring with the barrel, just leave the lid. If you leave the locking ring, someone can use a two-wheel dolly to steal it; without the ring, they can't tip it or the oil would spill. We've had theft problems, so yes, it can happen. Also, put your phone number on the barrel so the restaurant can call you when it's about three-quarters full. We also put a label on the barrel saying, "Waste Vegetable Oil Only — No water or trash, please; call when barrel is ¾ full, 555-1234."

You can usually obtain your drums for free, or at low cost. For open-top steel drums with no lids, try small oil companies. We get drums from them for free, and they even cut the tops out for us with a drum deheader. You'll have to clean a light film of oil out of them, though it's not hard to do. For a steel drum with a lid, try searching the yellow pages of the phone book or search the Internet for companies in your area. You can usually find drums for sale on eBay, but they may be too far away to pick up easily. You can usually find drums for free, or at low cost. We once ran a want ad and got several drums that way. We get our poly drums for free from a supplier of car-wash chemicals. They contained only car-wash fluids, so weren't difficult to clean before using. Such smaller drums work well for hauling oil from the restaurant barrels.

POLY DRUM

If you install some type of barrel filter on the drum, so as to limit the amount of food sludge you have to dispose of, you'll end up with cleaner oil. For ideas on filters and locking steel lids with built-in filters, see the Resources section.

Be prepared to have *twice as many drums* as locations to pick up. Reason: If you want the ease and convenience of swapping drums, especially in the winter, you'll need to take an empty one with you each time you go to pick up a full one. If you pump it out each time, and your oil never thickens in the winter, you won't need as many drums. You might try to get the restaurant staff to keep the drum of oil indoors to keep it from solidifying in the winter, as well as to reduce the incidence of theft or mischief.

HOW TO GET OIL OUT OF A 55-GALLON DRUM

Pumping it out: In the summer, pumping oil out of a large drum is our preferred method, because it's quick and fairly simple and doesn't involve lifting 400-lb. barrels of oil. We bought from an online source a gas-powered water pump that can also handle small solids; it can empty a 55-gallon drum in about 2 minutes. We originally built a setup of three 55-gallon MDPE drums that we took with us when doing this. We now use an IBC (intermediate bulk container) or tote like the one on the right. This tote will hold about 250 gallons and has a built-in 2-inch ball valve outlet on the bottom with a quick connect. Using this tote, we can pump the oil from the restaurant barrels into the tote at the site, and then empty it when back at the house or garage. This allows us to collect much more oil at a time, without having to swap barrels.

IBC TOTE

FOOT VALVE

Tip: If you pump into barrels, be extra careful not to overfill, or you'll have a "gusher" of oil coming out the second opening in your barrel and a huge mess to clean up. (It hasn't happened to us, but at a biodiesel conference I heard of such a gusher.)

Tip: Be sure to put a foot valve on the intake side of your oil pump. It usually has a screened intake, which will help you avoid sucking up large chunks of debris and keep your pump primed. If your oil has a lot of debris, you may need a secondary filter over the first to prefilter the oil for the smaller foot valve filter. We simply lower the secondary filter in just below the primary filter, using a wire handle on the secondary filter. Then have a bucket handy to put the dripping secondary filter into.

Pumping setup: For your pumping rig, there are several things to consider. Buy the most powerful pump you can afford, since oil can be very hard to pump with a weaker pump. Smaller, weaker pumps will wear out quickly, as they aren't rated to run continuously under heavy load for 15 to 20 minutes at a time. A pump will most likely pump at about half the rated flow rate, due to the high viscosity of the oil, lift height, and other factors.

In the photo below you'll see that we use heavy-duty suction hoses for both the intake and output sides. This works better, because the normal collapsible output hose is meant to be run straight, with no bends. Initially, we always ended up having to run the hose in such a way that we kinked it and had a hard time keeping the flow going. With the current hoses, we no longer have that problem. We've tried two types of hoses now and find that plain cooking oil will cause both to stiffen over a period of

GAS-POWERED OIL COLLECTION PUMP

about six months, requiring replacement. We'll be trying a new type of hose soon and will post results of that test on our website.

We also put a PVC pipe on the end of the suction hose, connected with quick connects (or camlock fittings), so that we can easily disconnect the intake tube to move the pump around. Using quick-

connect fittings on both the intake and output sides makes things much easier. You should put a "foot valve" on the intake side to keep the pump from losing the prime every time. A foot valve is basically a one-way valve that lets oil in but not back out.

Important point: If using quick connects, be sure to also get the quick connect caps and plugs so that you can plug hoses when not in use. If your oil is put directly into a barrel without filtering, you'll run into the sludge layer and start sucking up peanuts, food chunks, and other

CAMLOCKS, OR QUICK CONNECTS

debris, which can quickly clog the foot valve filter. So stay away from that layer, or use the secondary filter described in the tip box, or have the restaurant filter its oil as it goes into the barrel, or just

suck it up and filter it at home if your pump can handle the peanut-sized chunks.

A simple way to prefilter oil at home is to have an extra poly cone bottom tank for precisely that purpose. Then bring your oil home, pump it into the "settling" tank, and let it sit for a week or so in a warm location. In time, the heavier gunk will settle out and you can drain it off and get rid of it.

WASTE OIL HEATER
(COURTESY OF
MURPHYMACHINES.COM)

Tip: The oil you drain away with all the gunk in it can likely be burned in a waste oil heater after filtering out the particles. Such heaters can burn everything from waste motor oil and transmission fluid to biodiesel and waste vegetable oil. You can even heat your shop or garage with this waste oil! See the Resources section for vendors of these heaters.

Dolly it out: In winter we do it this way, using a trailer that rides

BARREL DOLLY

low to the ground. A full barrel can weigh about 400 lbs. and is extremely heavy to load with a two-wheeler (also called a dolly or a handcart). But it can be done much more easily with a dedicated barrel dolly, which has a special angle to it, custom feet, solid tires, and a simple clamp that hooks over the edge of the barrel. These work *much* better than a standard dolly. They're easier to tilt, load, and move. They're not cheap, but are worth it if you're moving much oil this way. This system also works for methanol drums.

If you wish to use a standard dolly, just get a strong dolly, a ratchet strap, and strong trailer ramps and then air the dolly tires up all the way. Note that longer trailer ramps and a low trailer make it much easier to do. Also, if possible, take a helper.

Lift it with a truck crane: You could put a small truck crane in the bed of your truck or trailer and then lift the barrel in using a

barrel-lifting device. Some who have tried this report that you *must* reinforce the bed of the truck or it will be bent. If using a trailer, you'll want to put a jackstand under one side when lifting to avoid bending the frame, unless you've got a superstrong trailer.

Scooping it out: You can scoop out the oil if it's very cold and solid. Yes, it's OK for it to solidify when it's cold

TRUCK CRANE

enough. It'll look really bad when it's cold, but don't worry about that if you've tested it and found it of acceptable quality. The scooping idea can be quite messy, however, so I don't recommend it.

A final note about collecting oil: Be extremely polite and responsible. You can build good rapport with your restaurant or other supplier by never letting their barrels overflow, by cleaning up the barrels (or swapping them out now and then), and by keeping the oil collection area clean. Always carry some type of oil-absorbing product, a broom and a dustpan, and some cleaner (such as Greased Lightning) to clean up any spills. Note that while sawdust will absorb most of the oil, it never gets it all, while a product designed just for oil spills will clean up the last little bit and leave your supplier happy. We even pick up trash in the area; that way, the owners stay happy, and we show them we appreciate being permitted to pick up their oil. Either you keep them happy or someone else will.

TESTING OIL ON SITE

Once you've located a new source for your used oil, the first thing you should do is ask them several questions about their oil. Ask a responsible person what goes into their oil barrels—is it mostly beef tallow from hamburger and such? If so, it will have a high gel point and may turn rancid quickly. You want oil that is mostly from fried foods, *not* beef tallow. Then find out how often they change their oil. If they are a typically busy restaurant, open for 3 meals a day, and change it less than every 7 to 10 days, be somewhat wary. Make sure they don't empty any water into their oil barrels, or dump excess food scrapings or chemicals. Some food chunks are normal, but if they put a lot of scrapings and other food debris in their oil barrels, you'll have a mess to sift through every time you get the oil. Basically, you want the oil to be mostly oil, not contaminants.

Then ask for a sample to test, and explain to them that not all oil will work for homemade biodiesel. Tell them you can perform a basic test in only a few minutes. Then if that passes, you'll need to test it more at home. The best way is to arrange for them to set aside a gallon or so for you to pick up later and test on site. You don't want to take a sample from the grease dumpster out back, as it will likely be terrible. When oil sits outside, it is deteriorating, building up the FFAs (free fatty acids), which makes for bad biodiesel. The oil in grease dumpsters is typically old and very high in FFAs.

Once you have some sample oil, you should perform *all* the following four tests, in this order: visual test, titration test, water test, and a minibatch test (all detailed below).

ITEMS TO TAKE FOR TESTING ON SITE
— A small burner of some type (a propane camp stove works well)
— Igniter for the stove
— A candy or meat thermometer
— A small pot
— A stirrer of some sort (a paint stirrer works well)
— Also, you may need a way to get the oil sample out of the barrel (turkey baster works well, or a small measuring cup or other device)

And you'll need your titration kit for the FFA testing (see Chapter 4).

VISUAL TEST

To test it, first inspect it visually to see if there's anything obvious about the appearance, or sniff it to detect a strong smell that indicates overused oil. The oil may range from golden in color and fairly clear, to dark amber and quite dirty, but don't worry too much about that now. You're looking for really nasty stuff like excess food gunk, water, and so forth. You might pour a quart or a gallon into a clear jug with a lid to allow you to visually inspect it, then if it looks fine, you can do a

CARBOY WITH A GUNK LAYER ON THE BOTTOM

titration test. If that passes, take the sample home and do a water test and make a minibatch with it for your final tests.

TITRATION TEST

The second test to do on a new source of used oil is a titration test. This is probably the most important test, since it will tell you how "used" the oil actually is. If it has been used for a long period, it will contain a lot of FFAs, which is bad for your biodiesel making. See Chapter 4 for extensive descriptions of how to do this test and what the numbers mean.

WATER TEST

First off, to answer your implied question: No, any water present in the oil *doesn't* simply boil out while the fryer is in use (even though a fryer is running much hotter than the boiling point of water). Food particles and other conditions help retain small amounts of water in the restaurant oil, so we all get stuck with some water whenever we pick up their free cooking oil. Water in oil can cause you to make more soap when making your biodiesel. It can also result in your making glop (a totally ruined batch) or an incomplete reaction, as compared to using a drier oil. You want oil that's as dry as you can get. There are ways to deal with some water in the oil, and I'll explain those methods later.

THE TEST

To test for water content, simply heat a small sample (a quarter cup or so) in a small pot, and see if it sputters or bubbles when it reaches the boiling point of water (212°F). **CAUTION:** You must stir it while heating, otherwise it can build up a steam pocket and suddenly erupt boiling oil all over you.

Note that *all* used oil will bubble and sputter. It's the amount of bubbling and sputtering that matters. Sorry, but there's no definitive way to describe exactly what's acceptable. Basically, if it really sputters and pops a lot, there's likely a lot of water in it. If it sputters just a little, it's probably really good. The way we learned is to test various oils from several restaurants, and then compare. Work carefully and cautiously, and keep notes.

You'll eventually learn the difference between oils. If you find one that doesn't sputter much at all, that's probably the best oil of all your options, in terms of the water content. But it still needs to pass the other tests before you can consider it good enough to use.

Also, don't worry about exactly when the bubbling starts. It'll depend on things like the size of your sample or the shape and thickness of your pot. *If* there's boiling at 212°F, you've got water. How much water is in your oil is up to you to learn. There really is no way to describe what's acceptable.

This test gives you only a basic idea of the water content, so use it, but don't necessarily rule out oil based on this test alone. The next test is more accurate.

QUANTITATIVE WATER TEST

There's another way you can measure the quantity of water in the oil.[63] In brief, you weigh it, heat it to drive out the water, weigh it once more, then do the math.

If you're going to perform a quantitative water test, you'll also need an accurate scale that can measure weight precisely, with a resolution of 0.1 grams (a tenth of a gram) or better. To do this test accurately, the scale should have an upper capacity of about 500 g or more. You could try it

SMALL, ACCURATE SCALE

with a top capacity of 100 g, but you'd have to use a much smaller sample, and you'd also lose some precision.

THE PROCEDURE

For this test it's advisable to wear safety glasses (hot oil can spatter and erupt with steam pockets), a long-sleeved shirt, pants, and leather gloves (to handle hot containers). And be *very* careful with hot oil, as it can seriously burn you, and can even catch fire if spilled on a hot stove.

1 Find a microwavable container such as a glass jar to put an oil sample in. Get something that's about ½ quart in size and heat resistant at the temperatures we're working with.

2 Weigh the empty container to the nearest tenth of a gram and record that somewhere.

3 Take a 300 to 400 ml sample of oil and place it in your container. The sample should be representative of all the oil you're going to react. Typically, I shake the oil up a bit, then I take the sample.

4 Weigh the sample in the container. Record this number. Subtracting the weight of the container gives you the actual weight of the oil. Record the oil weight. I designate this as the *"wet oil weight."*

5 Heat the sample in a microwave oven until the oil reaches a temperature of 250°F. IMPORTANT: You need to stir it often while heating to avoid steam pockets from erupting hot oil all over. Test the temperature of the oil periodically OUT OF THE MICROWAVE. Once you reach 250°F, keep it at this temperature until all boiling stops. You should heat for 1 or 2 minutes and then test the temperature. Then heat again at about 15 to 20 second intervals, and again check the temp.

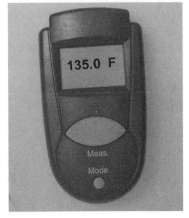

INFRARED THERMOMETER

6 Allow the sample to cool for 10 minutes or so. This allows any residual emulsified water to evaporate, plus it's safer. Stirring during this time will help ensure that all water escapes.

7 Weigh the sample again and record that number. Subtract the weight of the container. This is the oil's "*dry weight*." If you really want to be accurate, you'd do the whole heat/weigh thing again and again until the weight stops going down; this would assure you that all the water is gone. I think it's safe to make the assumption that if the sample has reached 250°F and there's no boiling, the water is gone. It's accurate enough for our purposes.

8 You can likely see where we're going. Take the wet weight and subtract the dry weight. The difference is the weight of the water that was in your sample. Now divide the water weight by the original "wet oil weight," which will give you the decimal fraction water content of the sample. Multiply by 100 to get the percentage.

Now you can determine whether the percentage of water is too much to deal with. You can "dewater" the oil at home, though there's a bit of a limitation to that. Also, because the water doesn't exactly drop out cleanly when you're dewatering, you end up with a sludgy oil that requires disposal. So I personally wouldn't pick up oil with more than about 2 or 3 percent water, as that would be more than 1 gallon of water for every 50 gallons of oil you process.

Tip: It's a good idea to check your thermometer for accuracy in boiling water, and confirm a boiling point reading of around 212°F. Some instruments are a mile off.

MINIBATCH TEST

Here you'll actually make a minibatch of approximately 750 ml of the sample oil. This test may uncover hidden chemical contamination or other nasties that could ruin your batch. If you can successfully make a minibatch, you should have no problems with a larger batch. If this test fails, however, you need to investigate the oil further before committing to it.

Remember, once you make a deal to pick up someone's oil, you need to be reliable. Canceling after committing to it is a pain for the restaurant owner or manager, so do your tests thoroughly before making any promises.

MINIBATCH WITH GLYCERINE
SETTLED OUT

STORING USED OIL

Once you get the oil home, you now have to figure out a way to store it. This could be simple for you, or it could be more complex. Here are some ideas that you may not have thought of.

Location: You can store your oil almost anywhere, but you'll probably want to store it out of sight of your neighbors. You really don't want someone calling the fire department (or Homeland Security!) on you because they're worried about what you're storing or what you're doing. This could potentially cause you problems. Your neighbors also might not like the looks or the location of your biodiesel setup. You might even want to take advantage of the sun to preheat your oil before you use it, so location could be another factor. And, of course, keeping the oil as close to the processing location can be helpful and a time-saver.

Containers: For simplicity, you can just store the oil in the containers you pick it up in. Then when you're ready to process it, pump it or pour it into your barrel heater or whatever. Or you can bring the oil home and pump it all into storage barrels, thus minimizing the number of half-full barrels sitting around. You can store it in MDPE plastic barrels, buckets, carboys, or steel drums. Some people put their oil into larger containers such as 275-gallon IBC totes, but that's up to you. As mentioned earlier, if you bring the oil home and pump it into a cone bottom tank, it will presettle out most of the gunk and (if warm enough) maybe some of the watery oil, too. Even if you store the oil in flat-bottom drums, the gunk will settle to the bottom, though in that situation there's a larger interface layer that prevents you from retrieving as much clean oil without getting into the gunk. The cone tank focuses everything, allowing for more efficient separation.

Solar preheating: You might be smart to take advantage of the sun to preheat your oil. In the winter this can make the difference between being able to pump it, or not. Otherwise, it can simply reduce the amount of time it takes to heat the oil, thereby saving on your energy bill. In the winter, the sun can help the oil presettle itself, as it won't settle out at all when it's very cold.

There are several ways that you can have preheating. First, you can simply paint your storage containers a flat black and set them in the sun. This method helps if you wait until later in the day to use your oil.

Another way is to build a simple, greenhouse-type room and store the flat black containers there. If you paint the solar box all black, you'll gain even more. Or you could have the walls covered in reflective material to reflect the sunlight back at the oil containers. You can get as complex as you want. It may even be possible to build a large enough solar heating room with black barrels of water to actually heat your biodiesel room. You'll want to study solar heating to do this, however, as you must observe a ratio of glass area to solar mass to make your system the most efficient. If there's too much mass, it won't heat up enough. If there's too little, it will reach maximum temperature too quickly and not be as efficient. Ideally, you want it to reach maximum temperature just before the sun sets. It will thus reach maximum thermal gain and will give back the heat all through the night, if desired.

The greenhouse is much more efficient at heating the oil than simply setting the painted barrels in the sun. *Note:* If you heat the oil this way for many months because you have excess oil, you *will most likely* be raising its FFA levels, which is not what you want. Therefore, limit the storage time to a few months, tops.

Tip: Double-paned glass loses less heat at night, as does an insulated box. The more thermally efficient the solar enclosure, the better it will heat the oil.

Be sure to store the oil where water won't get into the containers. Don't store it for any longer than you have to, as it may continue to get worse if stored for many months. Storing it for a few weeks actually helps, as the sludge settles to the bottom over time. I suggest marking all barrels with a permanent marker indicating the date you collected it, the restaurant or code name (for known-quality oil), and any other notes.

In the winter, use your best oils to obtain the best cold-weather performance. You'll know the best oils, as they will be liquid at colder temperatures, and will also test lower for FFAs. In the winter, it's not uncommon for some oils to become solid, but if your oil solidifies at higher temperatures you'll end up with fuel having a higher gel point.

UNDERSTANDING SAFETY ISSUES

The chemicals used to make biodiesel are considered to be extremely hazardous **if used improperly**. If you take the proper safety precautions, however, you can safely make biodiesel at home. To make biodiesel, you will be using two chemicals of concern. The first is a catalyst, such as lye or KOH. Both of them are caustic, meaning they can burn your skin, damage materials, and so on. Gloves and proper handling will protect your skin. More on these later.

The second chemical of concern is methanol. This can cause problems if you get it on your skin, and it's also flammable. Although methanol can be ignited, the EPA actually states that it is safer than gasoline in several ways. Here's the information from the EPA's own website:[64]

55-GALLON DRUM OF METHANOL

Methanol's fire safety advantage over gasoline stems from several physical and chemical properties:

Lower volatility—Methanol does not evaporate or form vapor as readily as gasoline does. Under the same conditions, exposed gasoline will emit two to four times more vapor than will exposed methanol.

Higher flammability requirement—Methanol vapor must be four times more concentrated in air than gasoline vapor for ignition to occur.

Lower vapor density—Gasoline vapor is two to five times denser than air, so it tends to travel along the ground to ignition sources. Methanol vapor is only slightly denser than air and disperses more rapidly to noncombustible concentrations.

Lower heat release rate—Methanol burns 25 percent as fast as gasoline and methanol fires release heat at only one eighth the rate of gasoline fires. These properties together make methanol inherently more difficult to ignite than gasoline and less likely to cause deadly or damaging fires if it does ignite. Methanol is the fuel of choice for Indianapolis-type race cars, in part because of its superior fire safety characteristics.

First I'll list some of the most important information taken from the MSDS (material safety data sheet) of the three chemicals we use that are the most dangerous. Information below is derived from the MSDS of these chemicals, but is not an exact quote, so you may want to look these up and print them yourself.

The biggest problem with methanol is fires. Storing excess methanol while handy is not the ideal thing to do. The safest way to deal with methanol is to purchase only what you need to make your batch. The National Fire Safety Code limits the amount of methanol you can store at a residential location to two 5-gallon containers. It's really not safe to store large amounts of methanol in your home.

If you don't have access to less than 55-gallon quantities, try to store the methanol outside or in a separate small ventilated room. If you sheetrock a room with two layers of $^5/_8$'' type X sheetrock, you will get a two-hour burn rating on the wall. You'll have to cover both sides of the walls, to protect the structural framing. Note that the drums that methanol comes in are extremely durable (if they're metal) and when all the lids are sealed, we've never seen one leak. I would find it hard to imagine that a drum in good condition would leak for no reason. The most common sources for leaks or spills are transferring the fluid to your methoxide (methanol and catalyst) mixer, and transferring the fluid from your methoxide mixer itself. Both can be minimized or eliminated through careful handling and mixing procedures.

The information below is believed to be accurate and represents the best information currently available to us. However, we make no warranty express or implied, with respect to such information, and we assume no liability resulting from its use. Readers should do their own research to determine the suitability of the information for their particular purposes.

Lye

Also known as caustic soda, Red Devil lye, NaOH, sodium hydroxide, and more.

SPILLS OR LEAKS OF LYE

Absorb any spills with an absorbent such as sand, vermiculite, fuller's earth, etc. After absorption, place in plastic bags for later disposal.

DANGERS TO SKIN AND ORGANS

Lye is highly corrosive. If you get it on your skin, it causes severe burns. May cause serious permanent eye damage. Very harmful by ingestion. Harmful by skin contact or by inhalation of dust.

FIRST AID MEASURES

Inhalation—Remove the affected person to fresh air. If breathing is difficult, they may need oxygen. You may need to call a physician.

Ingestion—Do not induce vomiting! You should give large quantities of water or milk if available. Remember the common sense rule to never give anything by mouth to someone who is unconscious. Get medical attention immediately.

Skin Contact—If you get lye on your skin, it's usually recommended that you should immediately flush the skin with water for at least 15 minutes, and remove contaminated clothing and shoes. Call a physician immediately. Dispose of clothing, or wash it before using again.

Eye Contact—In the event of contact with your eyes, immediately flush your eyes with water for at least 15 minutes, lifting both your upper and lower eyelids occasionally. And of course, get medical attention immediately.

FIRE SUPPRESSION FOR LYE

Lye is noncombustible; therefore, use the agent most appropriate to extinguish the surrounding fire. Do NOT get water inside containers because of the violent reaction lye has with water.

KOH

Also known as potassium hydroxide and caustic potash

See the above section for lye, as the properties of lye and KOH are very similar. Treat any accidents for KOH the same as you would for lye.

Methanol

Also known as carbinol, methyl hydroxide, wood alcohol, wood naptha, and wood spirit

Methanol is a poison! It can't be made nonpoisonous. It can cause eye and skin irritation, and can be absorbed through your skin or through breathing the vapors. In both vapor and liquid form it is flammable. Can cause central nervous system depression. Can also cause digestive tract irritation with nausea, vomiting, and diarrhea. May causes respiratory tract irritation. Large amounts may cause liver, kidney, and heart damage.

To avoid static spark explosions, you should always ground and bond containers when transferring methanol.

SPILLS OR LEAKS OF METHANOL

Absorb any spills, using an absorbent material such as sand, vermiculite, or earth. Don't use materials that are combustible (sawdust, paper, and so on). Be aware of any sources of ignition during cleanup, and avoid creating or causing any sparks. You can use a water spray to disperse the gas/vapor, though this may not prevent ignition in smaller, closed spaces. Be sure to provide adequate ventilation safely (but don't just put a sparking fan motor in the room). A vapor suppressing foam may be used to reduce vapors.

POTENTIAL HEALTH EFFECTS OF METHANOL

Eyes—Irritates the eyes, characterized by a burning sensation, redness, tearing, inflammation, and possible corneal injury. May also cause a painful sensitization to light.

Skin—Causes moderate skin irritation. It may be absorbed through your skin in harmful amounts with repeated or prolonged exposure. Long-term contact may cause defatting of the skin and dermatitis (will dry your skin out very easily).

Ingestion—If swallowed it may be fatal or cause blindness. May cause gastrointestinal irritation with vomiting, diarrhea, and nausea. Methanol may cause central nervous system depression, characterized by excitement, followed by headache, dizziness, drowsiness, and nausea. Advanced stages may cause collapse, unconsciousness, coma, and possibly even death due to respiratory failure. May cause cardiopulmonary system effects.

Inhalation—May cause respiratory tract irritation. May cause visual impairment and possible permanent blindness. May cause effects similar to those listed above, for ingestion.

Chronic—If you are exposed to methanol for longer periods, it can cause dermatitis. Breathing methanol for longer periods, or over longer periods of time, can cause effects similar to those of acute inhalation and ingestion. Long-term exposure may cause liver, kidney, and heart damage. Exposure can be cumulative—meaning that it builds up over time, so be careful about long-term exposure, too.

FIRST AID MEASURES FOR METHANOL

Eyes—Immediately flush eyes with plenty of water for at least 15 minutes, lifting the upper and lower eyelids now and then. Get medical aid immediately.

Skin—Immediately flush skin with lots of soap and water for 15 minutes while removing contaminated clothing and shoes. Get medical attention if irritation develops or persists. Wash clothing before reuse.

Ingestion—Here's the technical MDSD treatment: If the person is conscious and alert, give 2 to 4 cups of milk or water. Again, never give anything by mouth to an unconscious person. Seek medical aid immediately. Induce vomiting by giving one teaspoon of syrup of ipecac.

One interesting remedy for treating methanol poisoning, as listed on numerous websites, is by ingesting ethanol (nondenatured). Since most alcoholic beverages contain ethanol, many people keep some form of ethanol nearby to treat themselves in the event of a methanol contamination. Ethanol treatment works by means of competitive inhibition, meaning that it competes with the methanol in your system so that it's excreted by the kidneys rather than being transformed into a toxic byproduct.

Inhalation—Immediately move the person to fresh air. If they are having trouble breathing, give them oxygen. Get medical aid immediately. Do NOT use mouth-to-mouth resuscitation. If they quit breathing, give artificial respiration using oxygen and a mechanical device such as a bag and a mask.

FIRE SUPPRESSION FOR METHANOL

Methanol vapors may form an explosive mixture with air! Vapors can travel to a source of ignition some distance away, and flash back. For small fires, use a dry chemical, water spray, carbon dioxide, or alcohol-resistant foam. Use a water spray to cool containers exposed to fire. Water may be ineffective at putting the fire out.

RECOMMENDED SAFETY GEAR

To be safe when making or handling any of the chemicals listed above, it is **IMPERATIVE** that you wear the following safety items **AT ALL TIMES.**

Gloves—Chemically resistant gloves that come up higher on your arm are recommended. Use gloves that are resistant to both caustics and alcohols.

Goggles or full face shield—To prevent splashing onto your face or into your eyes, where these chemicals do the most harm.

Chemically resistant apron—A full-length apron is best.

Respirator—Mainly this is to prevent breathing of dust from the lye or KOH. It also prevents methoxide and so on from splashing into or onto your mouth. Note: Even cartridge respirators don't stop methanol fumes for long. The safest thing to do is to limit the amount of fumes, and to never breathe them. That's why most people use a simple dust respirator, as your exposure to the dust is very brief, and with a properly designed system you shouldn't be breathing methanol fumes at all.

Long-sleeved clothing—To prevent chemicals from getting on your arms.

Enclosed shoes—To keep chemicals off your feet.

Pants—Full-length, not half-length shorts. Again, you don't want any body parts exposed when you're working with chemicals.

Nearby water hose, shower, and so on—In the event that you should splash a large amount of chemicals on you. You could then quickly wash them off before they burn you.

VENTILATION

To avoid a buildup of vapors, it's important that you have adequate ventilation while handling lye, KOH, or methanol. Also, don't use or handle methanol near *any* ignition sources. Ignition sources could be a pilot light on a stove or heater, a sparking electrical switch, or the like. If you have room, you should preferably always keep your methanol *outdoors*, even when mixing the catalyst into it. Then plumb it back into the indoor area where your processor is, for safety.

Anytime you add a liquid to an enclosed tank, you have to displace an equal amount of air. That air is methanol laden and should be vented outdoors via some form of ventilation hose. Also, when you're mixing the methoxide in the oil, you may have a slight pressure buildup from the methoxide/oil reaction. Therefore, you must have a way to vent the air out of the tank. This air contains methanol fumes. A well-designed reactor is vented to the outside, away from your workspace.

SPONTANEOUS COMBUSTION

Store biodiesel, methanol, alcohol, and any flammable soaked rags in a safety can, to avoid spontaneous combustion.

Biodiesel-soaked rags should be stored in a safety can or dried individually to avoid the potential for spontaneous combustion. Biodiesel is made from vegetable oils or animal fats that can oxidize and degrade over time. This oxidizing process can produce heat. In some environments a pile of oil-soaked rags can develop enough heat to result in a spontaneous fire. This can also happen with rags soaked with any oily, combustible liquid.

Lesson Learned: Years ago, I had some oil-soaked rags (used to apply wood stain) spontaneously combust, so I know it can happen. I had foolishly left a small pile of oily rags on a cardboard box and they self-ignited during the night and burned through the floor of the house I was working on. If you don't have a safety can like the one pictured, dry oil-soaked rags individually (not piled up) in a well-ventilated area, on a noncombustible surface. Some people put them in a bucket of water. If you just throw them away, at the very minimum, store them away from structures.

OTHER IMPORTANT SAFETY NOTES

Many other potentially dangerous situations can arise when making biodiesel at home. In reality, many of us encounter similar situations daily when working on autos, small engines, using solvents and cleaners, and so on. The point is, we commonly do tasks around the house that could be dangerous if we fail to take proper safety precautions because we're rushed or simply not paying attention. By observing common safety procedures, and using our heads, we can be very safe.

Be careful about leaks in your system, for they can be leaking methanol-laden biodiesel into your workspace. Methanol seems to be especially prone to leaking, so watch your methanol mixer carefully.

Avoid having ignition sources near your processing area. If in doubt, turn them off before starting a batch. If you ever have a methanol spill, DO NOT turn off lights, open electric garage doors (except manually), and so forth. Take the same measures as you would in a propane or natural gas leak.

Never run a drill or other electric motor with exposed brushes in the vicinity of methanol. One of the older methods of making biodiesel involved mixing the oil and methoxide in a 5-gallon bucket with an electric drill (used by others, not us!). This method is extremely dangerous, as the drill could ignite the methanol fumes. I believe most people realize this now and avoid this method, but the technique is still cited on the Internet, so I feel I should point it out here. Use only well-sealed mixing containers.

Be aware that static electricity could ignite methanol. Static electricity can come from any two surfaces passing against each other, including your clothes, or even from fluid passing through a hose. Therefore, it's best to ground yourself with a grounding strap when working in the area of methanol vapors. You should also ground all methanol barrels, tanks, lines, and pumps, to help prevent static electricity. While I've never heard of anyone homebrewing biodiesel having a fire from this problem, fires have happened at commercial facilities when fuel was being unloaded.

Be careful to **use the correct gauge of wiring** and circuit breakers on your system.

Regularly inspect your clear vinyl hoses for signs of degradation. If you see them begin to crack, swell, delaminate, or harden, replace them at once. Instances have occurred of hoses rupturing, spewing the methoxide and biodiesel all over and injuring people. For this reason, our processors use extra-heavy wall hoses that we special order.

Make sure that your **vent hoses are clear** of obstructions and not kinked.

Provide adequate ventilation in the event that you have a methanol spill and need to quickly ventilate a room. If you have fans in the room, or fans that draw air into the room, they should be explosion proof. Another option is to force air into the room under pressure, from outside the room. Done properly, this should prevent any fumes from passing by the fan motor. Before you start handling methanol, you should start any fans.

If you choose to pump your methanol into any type of fuel can and do your mixing in that, or use the fuel can to add methanol to your actual mixer, you should do so outdoors, or in a room with no ignition sources nearby.

NOTICE: If you want to use a **respirator** to deal with the methanol fumes, you should know that the *only* kind of respirator approved for methanol is an *air-fed* model, meaning the respirator receives a flow of clean, filtered air from outside the room.

Always **watch your reactor for several minutes after starting** the mixing process to ensure that everything is going well and nothing's leaking.

When heating your oil, **keep the wattage low.** Look for heaters containing a "Low watt density" element. Elements that get too hot can actually cause the oil to catch fire, which I've seen happen. Better yet, use a barrel band heater like those listed in the Resources section.

If you use a **heating element in the oil itself,** you'll need to replace it every so often, because a heavy buildup can occur and cause the element to short out. Just keep an eye on it and replace it if it starts looking bad.

Keep several bags of Oil Dry, an **oil-absorbing product**, around, in the event of a spill. You'll want to contain it as soon as possible and then safely dispose of the Oil Dry. Be aware that even Oil Dry can spontaneously combust under the right conditions, so be careful when disposing of it. Sawdust works well for the initial cleanup of

plain cooking oil but not for methanol. Oil Dry works better for final cleanup.

Keep several large **fire extinguishers** nearby, in case a fire breaks out near your biodiesel and methanol area. I say "large" because small extinguishers have a short use time and might not suppress the fire before running out.

Take extra care to **store your chemicals safely,** since pets, animals, children, or an unsuspecting guest could inadvertently get some of the chemicals on them if you leave them dangerously exposed.

FINAL NOTE

In concluding the subject of safety, you'll probably be glad to learn that the finished product of biodiesel itself isn't considered hazardous. If you get it on your skin, it shouldn't burn or irritate. You can simply wash it off.

Also, it's very unlikely to catch fire because of its high flash point, and therefore can be safely stored in 55-gallon or larger containers. Its flash point is around 250°F—about twice as high as that of petroleum diesel. Flash point means the temperature that the fuel must reach to vaporize into a gas that can be burned. Thus, it's nearly impossible for biodiesel to catch fire from a casual spark or other incident. But if a fuel tank once contained unfinished biodiesel, it may also contain methanol fumes, which *are* explosive. Therefore, as a precaution, NEVER saw, cut, or weld on a steel tank that has ever had biodiesel or methanol in it unless you are certified to do so. People have died doing that, so don't risk it.

DOING THE TITRATION TEST PROPERLY

Titration is a laboratory procedure that allows us to determine the concentration of an unknown reagent using a standard concentration of another reagent that chemically reacts with the unknown. This standardized solution is called the "titrant." We need to have some way to determine when the reaction of the biodiesel will be complete. This completion is referred to as the "end point," or, more technically, as the "equivalence point." When that point is reached, all the unknown reagant has been reacted with the standard titrant, and some kind of chemical-indicator solution will let us know that.

Put more simply in biodiesel terms, titration basically tests the presence and concentration of FFAs (free fatty acids) in waste restaurant-fryer oil. (Titer comes from the French for "title," meaning identifying mark.)

Free fatty acids are a chemical component of the cooking oil (cooking oil is chemically known as a triglyceride). A triglyceride has a glycerine molecule as its base, attached to three long-chain fatty acids ("tri" meaning "three"). The more an oil is used, and the higher the temperatures it reaches, the more that some of its fatty acids will break off the triglyceride and end up as FFAs. The more FFAs there are, the harder the oil is to process because these FFAs form soap in the biodiesel-making process. The more soap that's made, the harder it is to wash. In addition, oil with a high FFA content won't fully convert, meaning that a lot of undesirable and harmful components are left behind. More on this later.

**Triglyceride Molecule
(Cooking Oil)**

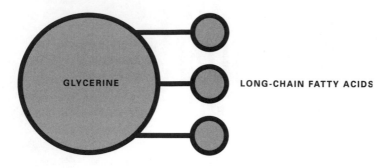

GLYCERINE

LONG-CHAIN FATTY ACIDS

The titration performs the catalyst/free fatty acid reaction on a very small scale, which we basically use pH value to measure. Some chemists before us have figured out that when *all* the FFAs have been turned into soap, the pH of the solution will rise to pH 8.5, which happens to be at the color change point of phenolphthalein indicator. We also use a homemade titrant made from the cooking spice turmeric. Turmeric indicator solution works the same as phenolphthalein. You can even use phenol red, though it's slightly less accurate.

WHY TITRATION IS NECESSARY

Simply put, the titration analysis is used to determine the free fatty acid content of the used cooking oil so that you'll know how much catalyst to add to your large batch to achieve a complete reaction.

Methanol and vegetable oil won't react to make biodiesel by themselves, so we have to add a catalyst to get things going. Because the excess FFAs *consume* some of the catalyst and end up making soap, we must add more catalyst that we basically sacrifice to the excess FFAs. If we add too much, we make even more soap—and risk a failed batch. Since we must know precisely how much extra catalyst to add, we do a titration test that measures the amount of FFAs in the oil.

A titration test takes less than a minute to do and is relatively simple, even though at first it may seem complicated. The test is

HOW THE BIODIESEL PROCESS TAKES PLACE

The biodiesel reaction needs a catalyst of either lye or KOH to cause the reaction to take place. During the reaction, the fatty acid molecules are broken off one by one. The methanol, in the presence of the catalyst, can then bond with this fatty acid to form biodiesel.

Once the first of the three fatty acid molecules breaks off and forms biodiesel, it leaves behind the glycerine molecule with two fatty acid molecules attached. It is now a diglyceride ("di" meaning "two"). We don't want this, so we continue the process and break off another molecule, leaving behind one molecule attached to the glycerine, which is what's called a monoglyceride ("mono" meaning "one"). Once that breaks off and forms a third biodiesel molecule, the glycerine molecule can settle out of the biodiesel and be drained off.

If you don't break off all the fatty acid molecules, you leave behind both monoglycerides and diglycerides, neither of which can be seen with the naked eye, but both of which can be harmful to your engine. So it's important to get the reaction to take place as fully as possible.

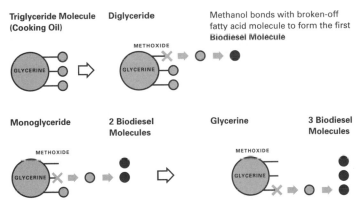

ILLUSTRATION OF THE TRANSESTERIFICATION PROCESS

UNDESIRABLE COMPONENTS IN BIODIESEL

This illustration shows a simple diagram of the undesirable mono- and diglycerides that can result from an incomplete reaction.

Monoglyceride showing
1 remaining fatty acid
attached to the glycerine

Diglyceride showing
2 remaining fatty acids
attached to the glycerine

LYE VS. KOH

When doing the complete reaction, you'll need to use as your catalyst either lye (sodium hydroxide, or NaOH) or KOH (potassium hydroxide). You can choose either one. Here are some things to consider, however, when making that choice.

LYE—Sodium hydroxide, better known as lye, used to be the most popular catalyst, mainly because you could go to the hardware store, buy some Red Devil lye, and make biodiesel with it. But lye is generally much more difficult to dissolve than are KOH flakes. The main advantage lye has is that it's usually cheaper, especially since it's generally purer than KOH, so even less of it is required. In small amounts it's also easier to find. Note that Red Devil lye is no longer sold, so it's getting harder to find, but there are other brands of pure lye available. Never buy lye that contains aluminum (as in Drano and similar products). Other considerations are that the glycerine can thicken more easily when made with lye, which can make it more difficult to drain, pump, or dispose of, especially in the winter.

Tip: Both forms of catalyst are highly hygroscopic (water absorbing). They will absorb moisture from the air to the point that they eventually dissolve in the water it absorbs. This property is called **deliquescence.** It is important to keep both catalysts in airtight containers and to reseal them as soon as you're done getting the chemicals out. If a catalyst absorbs moisture, it may be converted to sodium carbonate, which won't work any longer. Plus it will contain water, which of course is undesirable in a reaction.

KOH FLAKES

KOH—Potassium hydroxide, or KOH (sometimes known as *caustic potash*), is a little more expensive, but the glycerine will be more likely to stay runny and therefore easier to drain, pump, and dispose of. These properties can make KOH a lot easier to use, especially in cold winter months. Possibly the best reason to use KOH is that it dissolves *much faster* (provided that you use KOH *flakes*), typically in less than 5 minutes versus about 45 minutes for lye.

See the Resources section, at the end of this book, for places to buy your catalyst. You can also visit our website at *www.ezbiodiesel.com/bookbonus.htm* for clickable links to online sources of these chemicals. Using these links, you can have the catalyst drop-shipped directly to you, with no licensing required.

HOW TO TITRATE

Although you can perform a titration with any of three different indicator solutions, the best are phenolphthalein and turmeric. I will explain titrating using turmeric, as it is considered to be the best titrant, and you can make it at home.

Note: This procedure has been written for titrations using KOH. If you're going to use lye in the reaction, just substitute lye for the KOH in the directions.

TITRATION KIT

TITRATION KIT LIST
The ingredients below should be part of your Titration Kit. You might want to keep your supplies in a small toolbox so that you can carry it with you when out testing new sources of oil. Note that you can purchase complete titration kits containing everything you need to do a titration and also a

sample batch, except for the liquids. See the Resources section for information.

A – ISOPROPYL ALCOHOL

1 bottle—In the U.S., Iso-Heet Premium Fuel System Dryer and Antifreeze, 12 fl. oz. in the *red* bottle, is available at auto parts stores and is about 99 percent isopropyl alcohol. (*Note:* The yellow bottle of Heet is methanol, which you'll need for minibatches.) I've also purchased the alcohol at our local farmers co-op in the veterinary section, and even at big-box discount stores.

B – INDICATOR

Turmeric indicator solution, 1 small bottle (1 oz. is plenty)— Although I've mentioned that the test has to do with the pH of the test solution, others have learned that pH meters are poor substitutes for a simple indicator solution. Meters for testing pH require meticulous maintenance and constant recalibration using one standard pH solution to set the high end of the range and another to set the low end. Therefore, it's better to stick with the chemical indicator solutions.

C – CATALYST

KOH or lye, 1 gram for titrations—You may be able to find lye or its equivalent at most hardware stores or even some grocery stores. Be sure it's pure lye and doesn't contain aluminum or other substances. If in doubt, don't use it. If you can't readily find it, try a chemical supply business, which may require you to buy larger quantities. If you have a hard time purchasing it locally, see the Resources section or consider one of our Titration Kits, which comes with a sample of KOH (enough to do a titration and to prepare a minibatch). We now have a 29-minute video download available that details everything about the titration process. See the Resources section for more.

D – EMPTY 1-LITER BOTTLES

Bottles used to store 1 liter of the titrating fluid in and to make a minibatch in. New plastic or MDPE containers with tight-sealing lids are best (don't reuse containers that held other products, otherwise rinse them out well and allow to dry). Glass could break and can be dangerous and messy.

E – DISTILLED WATER

1 gallon of distilled water for making the titrating fluid (explained later in this chapter).

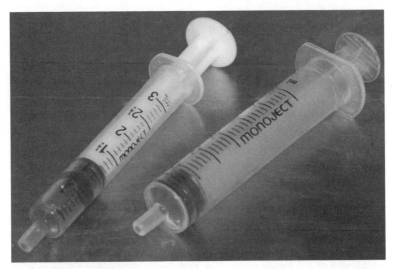

F – EYEDROPPERS OR SYRINGES

2 or 3—Eyedroppers are sold at drugstores and are graduated in ml (milliliters). They usually hold about 5 ml each and are graduated. You'll use one dropper to measure out some oil, another to measure out the titrant, and a third to dispense the alcohol. You should label them to avoid cross-contamination. Alternatively, try medicinal or veterinary **syringes** without the needles. A good place to find both syringes and eyedroppers is in the veterinary section at a farm and ranch store.

Tip: Syringes are marked in cc (cubic centimeter) increments, but 1 cc = 1 ml, so it works the same. You might want to buy a few extras, in case one acts up or quits working. Also, cooking oil can make the rubber in the syringe stick to the sides. Just leave the plunger extended, and the next time you use it you can push it in, freeing it up.

GRADUATED
CYLINDER

G – GRADUATED MEASURING CONTAINERS

You need a way to *accurately* measure 1 liter of distilled water. Graduated cylinders are perfect for this. Or you can use a large kitchen-measuring cup, but be sure it's accurate. The more accurate, the better. Graduated cylinders are the most accurate because they are tall and narrow. Tall,

LABELED TITRATION CONTAINERS

narrow containers measure much more accurately than short, wide ones (one reason that syringes are made long and narrow).

H – MIXING CONTAINERS

When titrating, we use three plastic-type storage containers. Or you can use small Mason jars. I suggest labeling them to avoid cross-contamination:

— Label one to use as the *titration container* that you do all your testing in.

— Label a second one for holding a small amount of the *reference solution* so that you can dip a syringe into it without contaminating the entire bottle.

— Label a third one to hold a small amount of the *alcohol* so that you can dip a syringe into this one also.

Note: Never pour unused titrant or alcohol back into the storage bottles, as that may contaminate your solutions. Instead, dispose of the leftover. If your containers have lids, though, you can just seal them until the next time. I like to keep another (labeled) container nearby just for pouring the junk fluids into when I'm done with them.

I – RAGS AND PAPER TOWELS

You can always use rags and paper towels when making biodiesel. You usually do a titration three times for accuracy, and can just use a clean rag or paper towel to wipe the titration container out between titrations.

J – SCALE

When mixing your titrating reference solution you'll need a scale that's accurate down to 0.1 g (1/10th of a gram) or finer. That accuracy is important, to avoid failed batches. Our first test batch failed due to our using a scale that was accurate only to 1 gram. The small scales that read up to around 200 grams work best for this. They're better suited than a larger scale at accurately measuring the 1g of catalyst for the reference solution. If you plan on making batches larger than 4 or 5 gallons, you'll probably want a second scale with a larger capacity but that is accurate to at least 1 g or better.

TIP: Buy some of the smallest Dixie cups to measure the 1 g of catalyst out. The reason is that the catalyst will often stick to other materials and is hard to empty all of it out, but it won't stick to the waxy Dixie cups.

WASH BOTTLE

K – WASH BOTTLE

Optional. Fill the wash bottle with alcohol and use it to dispense the alcohol into the graduated cylinder. This is quicker and easier than using a syringe or a pipette (also called a **pipet, pipettor,** or **chemical dropper**), which is a lab instrument used to transport a measured volume of liquid.

PREPARING THE TITRATION REFERENCE SOLUTION

This is a combination of distilled water and KOH (or lye). For simplicity, we will refer to using KOH, or just "catalyst." Titrating fluid is your reference fluid when doing titrations. It's made by dissolving 1 g KOH into 1 liter of distilled water. To make this solution, pour exactly 1 liter of distilled water into your container (which should be clearly labeled), then add exactly 1 g of KOH. Put the lid on tightly and shake the container until the KOH is completely dissolved. This liter will last quite a while, and you'll use small amounts of this fluid many times over the course of several months.

Accuracy is important, so if you don't have accurate scales, there's another way you can achieve this accuracy. First, measure out 10 g of catalyst and dissolve this into 1 liter of distilled water. Then take 100 ml of this water and mix with 900 ml distilled water.

You now have a very accurate ratio of 1 g catalyst in 1 liter of distilled water.

MAKING THE TITRATION INDICATOR SOLUTION

Although you can use a phenolphthalein indicator, for our purposes we'll use a turmeric indicator solution both because it's considered highly accurate and because you can make it with a cooking spice. You can purchase ground turmeric at most grocery stores or health food stores. Here are the details of how to make this indicator:

1   Thoroughly mix ground turmeric with 90 percent or better isopropyl alcohol in the following proportions: 1 part turmeric to 5 parts alcohol (it doesn't have to be exact).
2   Let the mixture settle until most of the turmeric has settled out.
3   Decant the liquid into a dispenser bottle with an eyedropper, pipette, or similar device. (Decant means to draw off the liquid, leaving the sediment behind.)

THE TITRATION PROCEDURE

This is the procedure using *turmeric* as your indicator. Note that this can seem slightly different than other methods you may have read about on the Internet. But if you look closely, it should be the same, *except* that we use double the usual amounts and then divide the results by 2, which gives a slightly more accurate reading (accuracy is important, to avoid failed batches). You could use 4x the normal amounts, and divide the results by 4, but we believe that using 2x and dividing by 2 gives accurate-enough results. Plus we incorporate a "blank titration" into the procedure, which is sometimes optional but still a good idea.

Note: When we speak of the turmeric's "changing color," we're looking for any color change, not a specific color change. The titrant will start out mostly colorless, but slightly yellow. When it changes color it may appear pink, purple, or red toned. As long as it changes color and holds that color for 15 seconds or longer, that's all that matters. It will often lose the color after 20 to 30 seconds, but that's OK. Don't look for a solid color, just a color change all throughout the liquid.

1 Using the **alcohol syringe or eyedropper**, draw up 20 ml of alcohol into the syringe and dispense it into the titration container. This doesn't have to be exact, as the alcohol is only a carrier. You can also dispense the alcohol into a small graduated cylinder, which is faster to use than refilling the syringe 2 to 4 times.

Tip: if using medical syringes, pull a small amount of air into the syringe first, then draw up the fluid until it's at the desired measurement mark. This makes it both easier to draw the fluid in and easier to read. In any graduated device (syringe, pipette, or similar), you should read the bottom of the curve of liquid.

---

2 Now add roughly 5 or 6 drops of turmeric indicator solution to the alcohol and swirl around well to mix.

3 Next perform a **blank titration.** This neutralizes any acid that may be in the alcohol, making the titration more accurate. Usually, it will take only a drop or two. If it starts going bad, it may take a dozen drops. When you're done, you've neutralized any acidity and the solution is ready to go.

4 To do this, fill one of the eyedroppers with some of the reference titrating fluid. Swirl the alcohol/turmeric mixture in the titration container, then slowly begin to add some titrating fluid to the mixture a drop at a time until the alcohol just starts to turn a permanent color all throughout, and then **STOP.** You're now ready to titrate the oil in question.

5 Using the other oil eyedropper, add to the alcohol exactly 2 ml of the oil to be titrated. Warm oil (above 100°F) is best, as it will dissolve in the alcohol more easily.

6 To warm the oil-and-alcohol mixture further, place the solution into a microwave oven and microwave until the first bubble appears (5 to 10 seconds), then STOP. Note that this step is not absolutely necessary if the ambient air temperature is above 60°F. If it's colder, the oil may not dissolve properly in cold alcohol, making heating necessary.

7   Now swirl the solution to mix the oil and alcohol together well. The mixture will be a murky yellow, but the exact color isn't important just yet.

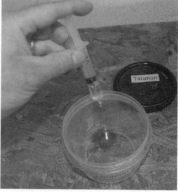

Tip: Never try to draw up exactly 1 ml of oil into an eyedropper or pipette, because you will find it difficult to get it all back out. Instead, draw up 3 ml, then squeeze out 2 ml, leaving 1 ml behind. This is much more accurate.

COLOR BEGINNING TO CHANGE DURING A TITRATION

8   Next, fill the **titration eyedropper** with exactly 5 ml of titrating fluid and start adding it, about ¼ ml at a time, into the titration container while swirling the mixture constantly. Keep swirling and adding drops until the entire solution changes color and lasts for 15 seconds or more while swirling. Keep swirling all the time, as it will often turn color, then back to yellow, until you've added enough to fully neutralize the FFAs. You may have to refill the syringe and continue adding more titrant with some oils. Just keep going until you get the desired color change. You should experiment with this in the beginning to know what to look for. If I were doing this for the first time, I would reach this point and then try adding more just to see what happens. You'll soon know what to look for.

9   Now, notice how many milliliters it took and **write that number down.** Since we're using double the normal amounts, you need to **divide this number by 2.** Write this final number down too, as this is your titration number.

10 To ensure accuracy, wipe the titration container out, then repeat the test once or twice more. Use the average reading from these tests as your final number.
    Example: If you do the above steps and you end up using 2½ ml of titrating fluid, you'd then divide that by 2, which would give you a final acid number of 1¼. That's the number you go by to determine how much lye to add to a larger batch.

Important: Your titration should be done with the same catalyst you're going to use to make your biodiesel. If you're using lye to make your fuel, use that to make your lye/water reference mixture. But if you're using KOH, use a gram of that to make a water/KOH mixture, instead.

As with reading and following any recipe, whether for a fancy cake or a chemical mixture, I know it seems difficult at first. Once you've done it a few times, it gets easy. Really, all you need to remember is this:

20 ml alcohol, 5–6 drops indicator, 2 ml oil, 5 ml titrant

HOW TO USE THE TITRATION INFORMATION

The titration will give us a number (technically called acid value or acid number).

We know that the free fatty acids will consume some of our catalyst during the biodiesel-making process, so we compensate by adding a specific amount of catalyst to "sacrifice" to the free fatty acids so that the rest of the catalyst can continue the biodiesel reaction.

For every 1 ml titration result (that is, the acid number), you'll need to add an extra 1 gram of lye (on top of the base amount) for each liter of oil/FFA you're reacting. This is to compensate for the side reaction caused by the FFA content. But don't worry, you really don't need to do any math. To simplify things, just use the KOH calculator in the back of the book, or use the biodiesel calculator available for download on our website.

WHAT'S CONSIDERED GOOD OIL?

If your titration results are in the range of 0 to 3 ml, that's considered "good" oil. From 3 to about 5 or 6 ml is considered poor but usable. Over 6 ml is getting questionable and should be avoided until you gain more experience. "Average" restaurant oil will require about 2 to 3 ml on the titration, while really bad fast-food grease can take 10 ml or more, which is completely unusable with a transesterification alone. Using oil this bad requires first processing with an esterification, which involves an acid pretreatment followed by a normal transesterification. An esterification adds a lot of work and complexity to the whole process, and we won't go into that in this book. If you want to use the better oil, go for a titration value of under 2½ or 3 ml.

THE FINAL STEP: DO THE MATH

To calculate the amount of lye to use, **I highly recommend using either the KOH calculator in the back of the book, or the free biodiesel batch calculator,** which is available on our website at *www.ezbiodiesel.com/bookbonus.htm* (in the links section). This will eliminate the possibility of making a math mistake and ruining a batch because of that. Plus, that way you can skip the next few pages and save yourself some grief.

If you want to do the math yourself, here's how to calculate it for a test batch of 1 liter. All figures are assuming you're using lye. Using the *final acid number*, each 1 ml of titrating fluid used corresponds to 1 **extra** gram of lye you'll need to add (on top of the base of 5 g) when making your liter batch, simply to eliminate the free fatty acids in that oil. So if your final acid number came to 1.25, you'd add that to the base amount of 5, giving you a result of 6.25. Now multiply that by the number of liters, which is 1 in this case. This gives you a result of 6.25, which is how much lye to add to this batch.

WORKING WITH BATCHES LARGER THAN 1 LITER

When you've bought or built a biodiesel processor and want to make more than one liter at a time, you will use the same calculations, but here are a few more.

First off, for simplicity, we'll do everything using metric calculations, since we've been talking in liters and grams already.

If you only know the gallons you're using, you can convert the amount of oil you're using to liters by multiplying the gallons times 3.8.

Example: 10 gallons U.S. = 38 liters

To calculate the methanol needed, multiply the amount of oil being processed by 0.22 (that is, 22 percent). You *might* get by with lower amounts, but we use an amount on the high side (as recommended for homebrewers by the University of Idaho) because it helps ensure a complete reaction. This approach works by preventing the reaction from reaching equilibrium and stalling out. Having excess methanol keeps the reaction pushed to the correct side, which is where the reaction is taking place.

Example: 76 liters × 0.22 = 16.7 liters, or 4.4 gallons of methanol (16.7 / 3.8)

All this converting can get confusing, which is one reason I highly recommend the biodiesel batch calculator on our online spreadsheet. It comes in especially handy if you use a catalyst that isn't 100 percent pure since it will automatically adjust for the purity of your catalyst.

FOR KOH

When using KOH, you do the same calculations. Take the final number you got with your titrant solution calculations and add that to the base amount. Using KOH instead of NaOH (lye), you'll have a different "base" quantity for the reaction. You'll use **7 grams per liter instead of 5.**

KOH EXAMPLE

Using our example above, the final titration number showed 1.25 ml. That means that, to make biodiesel, we'll need 1.25 **extra** grams for each liter of oil we're reacting. If we're making 76 liters of oil (equal to 20 gallons U.S.), then your calculations would look like this:

7 grams per liter base amount + 1.25 extra grams needed = 8.25 grams per liter
76 liters oil × 8.25 = 627 grams of KOH needed (assuming a 99% purity)

To calculate the methanol needed, multiply the amount of oil being processed by 0.22 (22 percent). Use the same conversion for lye.

Example: 76 liters × 0.22= 16.7 liters, or 4.4 gallons of methanol (16.7 / 3.8)

To make it even more confusing, KOH comes in a variety of purities, and you have to adjust your calculations for that. If your KOH is less than 99 percent pure, you'll need to divide the catalyst result (above) by the percent purity.

Example: Divide 627 by 0.90 for 90 percent purity.

The biodiesel calculator will adjust for the purity, so if you're going to use KOH, use our calculator. The good news is, you won't have to adjust the mix of the titration reference solution! The titration will automatically reflect the impurity level for you.

BETTER TITRATION TESTING EQUIPMENT

If you're ready to begin doing even more accurate titration tests, or you'd like to speed the process up, consider upgrading your testing equipment.

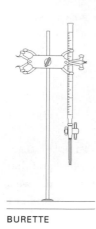

BURETTE

The easiest way to do this is to purchase a burette and a stand (or build the stand yourself). A self-zeroing burette is the key piece of labware you'll need for a highly accurate, easy-to-use titration station. The burette is a graduated cylinder that gives a reading accurate to 0.1 milliliters. It's easily refilled and it always resets itself to zero. During titrations, you simply open the burette's valve, allowing the titrant to slowly drip into your sample. There's no need to count drops, because when your titration goes to completion you simply read your result from the gradations marked on the cylinder. The process is fast, which enables you to easily perform several titrations that can then be averaged, assuring you of using the correct amount of catalyst for your biodiesel transesterification.

The preparation of titrant (commonly 1 g lye or KOH per 1,000 ml water) and the preparation of the sample (typically 2 ml of oil in 20 ml isopropyl alcohol) remains the same process as you'd normally use. The burette replaces the eyedropper used to perform titrations.

MAKING TEST BATCHES, THEN LARGER BATCHES OF BIODIESEL

Before you consider plunging in and making a big batch of biodiesel, you should first try making a small, 1 liter test batch. This way, you'll get a feel for the entire process and won't have to risk ending up with a 20-gallon batch of glop (thick, totally unusable, failed biodiesel). Plus, you'll get to see the process in action, since you'll do it in a small, clear container and can see what's going on during the various steps. I recommend that you do this for each **new oil source**, before venturing to make a large batch with it.

Note that the methods detailed below are meant only to demonstrate how the process works, not to make high-quality fuel. They'll let you see the oil actually separate into distinct layers of biodiesel and glycerine.

THE BLENDER METHOD OF MAKING TEST BATCHES

Once a popular method, the blender method is no longer recommended, primarily for safety reasons. Kitchen blenders can leak, throwing a caustic oil mess all over. Instead, I suggest that you try the bottle method (page 98). Also, be sure to do it somewhere like your garage, as a spill of the methoxide can ruin such things as countertops and carpets.

THE BOTTLE METHOD OF MAKING TEST BATCHES

MATERIALS REQUIRED
— 1 liter of oil (new or used)
— Lye (you'll need at least 6 g)
— Methanol (at least 250 ml);
  Heet Gas-Line Antifreeze in the
  yellow bottle is methanol, and
  it's easy to find in most auto
  supply and big box stores in
  the United States
— Titration kit (as described in
  Chapter 4)

YELLOW BOTTLE OF HEET-
CONTAINING METHANOL

EQUIPMENT REQUIRED
— 2-liter soda bottle in sound condition with a top, and *dry* inside
— Accurate measuring cup, beaker, or the like, to measure out 250
  ml methanol
— Scale to measure 6 g lye, accurate to 0.1 g
— Container to mix the methanol and lye, which makes methoxide;
  it needs to have a secure, leakproof lid, and have a capacity of at
  least 300 ml
— Funnel

THE TECHNIQUE
Follow the directions carefully, and you'll produce a respectable batch of biodiesel. Practice makes perfect.

HEAT THE OIL

If using *waste oil*, take 1 liter and heat to at least 240°F to remove all water (heat in something like a pot or glass container, not the plastic soda bottle). If water is present, the oil may pop and splatter, so be careful. Also, be sure to stir occasionally while heating, to avoid steam pockets, which can explode. Once the water is gone and the oil becomes calm and quits popping, let it cool to 130°F.

If you're using new oil from the bottle, it should have no water in it, so in this case just heat to 130°F when you're ready to mix the methanol and lye.

MIX THE METHANOL AND LYE

While waiting for the oil to cool, mix your methanol and lye (NaOH) to make the methoxide. Use 250 ml of methanol. This is a little more methanol than some people use, but it'll help to ensure a successful first batch.

If you're using *new oil*, this will require 4 g lye (NaOH).

For *used oil*, you should do a titration to determine the correct amount of lye (NaOH) to use. However, if you don't have the materials to do a titration, just use 6 to 7 g lye (NaOH), as this amount almost always works. If you don't have a scale, this is about 1 level teaspoon measure (metric or imperial). (Mark that teaspoon and never use it again for anything but biodiesel, or just use a plastic spoon, then throw it away.)

If you use lye, you'll find the lye and methanol difficult to mix, so you'll have to work at getting them to mix completely. And remember, *don't sniff the fumes,* as they're dangerous. Also, CARTRIDGE RESPIRATORS DO NOT WORK WITH METHANOL. You basically want to avoid the possibility of methanol fumes as much as possible, and if you do get around them, just don't breathe while you are directly over open methanol.

To speed things up, start with the methanol at about body temperature (but not warm). When you mix the two ingredients, the temperature may increase quite a bit—this is normal. Make sure *all* the lye is dissolved. This could take 10 to 15 minutes or more, but don't rush it. You may need to crack the lid and vent the pressure occasionally while mixing.

After *all* the lye has dissolved, make sure you still have 250 ml methanol, as some evaporation may have occurred during mixing. If not, just add enough to bring it back to that level.

MAKING THE BIODIESEL

— When the oil's temperature has dropped to 130°F or slightly less, use a funnel to pour the liter of oil into a *dry* 2-liter soda bottle or similar bottle with a good lid.

— Now take the lye/methanol mixture, which is commonly called methoxide by biodiesel homebrewers, and carefully pour it on top of the oil, using the funnel. (Avoid spills, which can damage skin and surfaces.)

— Screw the top on *tightly* and shake vigorously for about 60 seconds. Again, you may want to vent pressure occasionally, but keep the lid on the rest of the time.

THE RESULTS

After shaking the bottle, just put it down and observe. The oil will begin to change color and probably will have a rolling action to it. It should change color from a chocolate milk shade to a darker brown, depending on the type of oil you're using.

Then in around 10 minutes, and almost as if by magic, you'll see it start to settle into two distinct layers. The bottom layer will be the waste byproduct of glycerine, while the top layer will be biodiesel. The bottom layer will continue to settle and build up for hours, but the majority will settle out within about an hour or so. This is referred to as separation.

If you watch carefully, after a while you'll see a very definite and slowly sinking line moving toward the top of the biodiesel as the glycerine slowly settles. It will seem as if the biodiesel is appearing on the top, as if by an optical illusion, but in reality the glycerine is simply settling out of the biodiesel.

After about a day, you should now have a bottle containing lighter colored biodiesel on top of a layer of darker glycerine. The biodiesel may be quite cloudy, and it will take a few days for it to clear more.

You will usually end up with about the same amount of glycerine as the amount of methanol that you put into the bottle. The conversion ratio is around 98 percent.

WASHING THE BIODIESEL TEST BATCH

Now that you've made your first batch of biodiesel and it's settled for a day or two, it's time to wash it, if you wish. Doing so isn't really needed for this test batch, but it can be done if you like, for practice.

You can wash a small batch like this by using an extremely simple method. It involves five washes, but can usually be done in less than an hour.

Normally you wash biodiesel because unwashed biodiesel contains soap. Be aware that if you agitate your first few washes too vigorously, there's a real chance that the water, soap, and biodiesel will form an emulsion that may take days or even weeks to separate.

Therefore, it's very important, whether with large or small batches, to start out *extremely gently.*

To begin, you first need to drain the glycerine. You can do so by turning the bottle upside down with your thumb or finger over the opening. Then just allow the glycerine to drain until only biodiesel remains. You can now begin the wash process, below.

WASH #1
— Gently pour about 500 ml of warm (around body temperature) water into the bottle.
— Put the top back on tightly.
— *Gently* rotate bottle end over end for about 30 seconds.
— After 30 seconds, set the bottle upright on a table.
— If you have been *gentle*, the water and biodiesel will separate immediately. The water won't be clear, but rather will be milky looking.
— Remove top and, using your thumb as a stopper, turn bottle upside down and drain the water, using your thumb as a valve.
— You've finished the first wash.

WASH #2

— Pour in another 500 ml water and repeat the first wash routine, except rotate *gently* for about 1 minute.
— Drain the same way you did in the first wash.
— You've completed the second wash.

WASH #3

— Do this wash exactly as you did wash #2.

WASH #4

— Same as washes #2 and #3, but using a little more agitation. Then drain as usual.

WASH #5

— Same as wash #4, but on this final wash shake vigorously and then drain.

TESTING FOR COMPLETION

Washing is finished when, after shaking, the water is nearly clear. Notice that in the later washes you should be able to shake much more vigorously. The water and oil will take a little longer to separate because the water will form tiny bubbles in the biodiesel that take time to settle out.

BIODIESEL WASH STAGES: UNWASHED, WASHED, DRIED

Washed biodiesel will still be very cloudy and a lot lighter colored than the original biodiesel. Let it sit with the biodiesel exposed to air for a few days to dry the remaining water out of it. After a few days of settling and drying, it will clear up.

MOVING ON TO LARGER BATCHES

If you're ready to move up to making larger batches of biodiesel, the first thing you need to consider is equipment. You obviously don't want to try making 20 gallons, one liter at a time, so you need to consider investing in larger equipment.

To do this, you have several options, which I'll outline here. I won't suggest which method you should use, because that's up to you to determine, based on your skill level, personal preference, space and facilities, time, patience, and money. Instead, I'll outline the pros and cons of each. See the Resources section for more information on available kits and processors.

OPTION 1—DESIGN IT YOURSELF

You can study all the biodiesel processor designs out there, and then, using that information plus the information and resources in this book, you could design your own from scratch. Many people have done that successfully. It's *not at all easy*, but it can be done.

PROS

— The cheapest way to get started. You'll likely spend from $600 to $1,200 building your own processor, depending on the design you come up with.
— Satisfaction of doing it yourself.
— You'll understand the design well, this way. Allows for easier future modifications.
— Can build a system that fits your specific needs.

CONS

— You'll probably end up spending over a hundred hours studying other designs, figuring your design out, acquiring all the parts, and finally assembling it.
— Most people end up taking from several weeks to several months to complete a processor. Our first processor took a month or more to figure out the design, then another three weeks just to build it (with all the hardware store trips), then we modified it about seven or eight times over several months.
— You'll probably have to modify your design several times to get it right.
— I can pretty much guarantee that you'll make *dozens* of trips to the hardware store to do it this way, and still won't find everything locally.
— Most likely you'll have to order some items on the Internet or from another source.
— Takes the most time of all the methods.
— May be beyond your skill level.

— There are numerous processing principles that are very important to follow, and most people who design their own processor leave out one or more of these because they don't know better. If you plan on designing your own, study this book thoroughly and make sure you incorporate all its principles in your design, otherwise you'll be making low-grade fuel.

— No technical support from a manufacturer, so you're on your own when (not if) you encounter problems.

— Easiest to make dangerous mistakes this way, which could result in serious bodily harm, or worse. Also could result in fires, explosions, and the like, if not done correctly.

— Could cost a lot more than buying a professionally designed processor, after engine repairs, wasted parts, lost time, and other side effects.

OPTION 2—BUY A DO-IT-YOURSELF GUIDE

You can buy a complete set of instructions that will detail how to build your own biodiesel processor. You simply *supply the labor and buy all the materials.* The design and construction details are all provided. This is a great time-saver for the do-it-yourself person. *The main difference between this and Option 1 is that you don't have to design it yourself.*

PROS

— This can save you a lot of time over designing a processor yourself. It could literally save you from a dozen hours, to 60 or more.

— Prevents a lot of frustration if you don't want to (or can't) figure out your own design.

— Requires less skill to build than designing your own from scratch.

— You still get to build it yourself, so you have the satisfaction of putting it together with your own hands.

— There are several do-it-yourself designs available on the Internet.

— A little more affordable to build than a ready-to-run processor

— Less chance of building a dangerous processor this way.

CONS

— Costs more than doing it all yourself.

— Still takes more time than buying a ready-to-run processor.

— Requires many trips to the hardware store, auto supply shop, and so on, but less time than Option 1.

— Some kit instructions are vague and difficult to understand.

— Technical support may be quite limited.
— Many kits are poorly designed or leave out important processing instructions and design criteria that enable you to make high-quality fuel. If you're new to biodiesel, you probably won't recognize these facts until you've bought a kit and built it.
— There are many biodiesel processors on the market. Many kits are put together by people who lack a thorough understanding of how to make high-quality fuel, and don't know the difference between high-quality fuel and fuel with excess glycerine, monoglycerides, or diglycerides (all of which will cause you problems). Do you want to risk this? There are numerous processing principles that many kit or processor builders leave out, to save money. Study this book instead, and make sure they incorporate all its principles in their design, otherwise you'll just be making low-grade fuel. If the seller doesn't describe what safety features they incorporate into their kit, you could end up with a dangerous processor.
— Only a few designs are available for purchase this way. The two designs I've seen are the Appleseed, and an Appleseed variant made from 55-gallon drums.

OPTION 3—BUY A "KIT" WITH INSTRUCTIONS AND PARTS

With this option, you purchase a kit with the complete assembly instructions *plus* all the parts to build it. The main difference between this option and Options 1 and 2 is that you not only don't have to design the processor, you also don't have to run all over the county trying to find the parts.

PROS
— Saves even more time than Options 1 or 2.
— Prevents a lot of frustration if you don't want to spend forever chasing down the parts to put your own processor together.
— You can begin building it the same day.
— Requires less skill to build than designing your own from scratch.
— Doesn't require you to figure out what everything is, as you would with Option 2. For example, you may not know what a check valve is, or a cross, or a union. A well-designed kit will have everything clearly labeled so that you can easily identify the parts.

— You still get to build it yourself, so you have the satisfaction of putting it together yourself.

— Numerous "kits" are available on the Internet. Our kits actually come preassembled. You simply install the assemblies on the tank, hook up some hoses and wiring, and you're done. This is hands down the simplest method of building your own processor.

— Still a little more affordable than a ready-to-run processor.

AN ASSEMBLED APPLESEED KIT
(PHOTO COURTESY GRAYDON BLAIR,
UTAH BIODIESEL SUPPLY)

— You still get the satisfaction of building it yourself, but with much less frustration. I can guarantee you that there are a lot of half-finished processors out there, as many people get halfway into designing and building their own and realize they really don't know what they're doing. You'll save yourself some frustration with a kit.

— You'll likely get better customer support with a kit. (For example, we back ours with unlimited support and a one-year guarantee on parts.) Look for both in any kit you consider.

— Less chance of building a dangerous processor this way.

CONS

— Costs more than Options 1 and 2.

— Still takes more time than buying a ready-to-run processor.

— Some kit instructions are vague and difficult to understand. Be sure the kit you buy has written and illustrated instructions, if you don't want to become extremely frustrated.

— Again, many kits are poorly designed or leave out important processing instructions and design criteria that enable you to make high-quality fuel. If you're new to biodiesel, you probably won't know until you've bought and built the kit.

— There are many biodiesel processors out there. Many kits are put together by people who don't have a thorough understanding of how to make high-quality fuel, or don't know the difference between high-quality fuel and fuel with excess glycerine,

monoglycerides, or diglycerides (all of which will cause you problems). Do you want to risk it? There are numerous processing principles that many kit or processor builders leave out, to save money. Study this book, and make sure they incorporate all its principles in their design, otherwise you'll be making low-grade fuel.
— If the seller doesn't describe what safety features they incorporate into their kit, you could end up with a dangerous processor.

OPTION 4—PURCHASE A READY-TO-RUN PROCESSOR

With this option, you purchase a processor that's completely assembled and ready to go. After you do some minor setup, you can begin making biodiesel right away. That's assuming that you have everything else you need, such as used oil, methanol, lye, barrels, and other equipment.

PROS
— Saves the most time of all. You can actually begin making biodiesel the same day you get it, *if* you've studied a book like this one, *and* if you have in place everything else you need. You might require an electrical circuit, or some barrels, for example. We'll list these kinds of items later in the book so you can see what else you might need if you buy a ready-to-run processor.
— Prevents a lot of frustration if you don't want to spend forever designing a system, and then forever chasing down the parts to put your own processor together.
— Requires little or no skill to get it going. You'll probably have to do some minor setup before you can get started.
— Numerous ready-to-run processors are available on the Internet. In our line of biodiesel processors, we have many models of ready-to-run processors available, ranging in size from a small, homeowner size, 20 gallons per batch output to a commercial sized, 5,000 gallons per batch output. You can view them at *www.ezbiodiesel.com/bookbonus.htm.*
— They are usually put together cleanly, and look more professional than most people's homemade processor designs. We've seen some really scary-looking homemade processors out there, built by people who've never built one before.

— Will pay for itself in savings in less than six to eight months for most people. If you have two diesel vehicles or drive more miles each month than average drivers, the processor pays for itself about twice as fast.

— The design work is already done, and, if the processor was designed properly, you won't risk ending up with low-grade fuel, as you would with a homemade unit.

— Usually comes with all the important items you need to make biodiesel (varies with the manufacturer; see our list on page 222). This will save you a lot of time trying to figure out where to get the titration equipment, scales, plumbing parts, tanks, drying units, pumps, heaters, filters, and on and on.

— Safest processor design (this can vary, however, so do your homework when shopping).

— Best technical support option (again, varies with the manufacturer, but we offer lifetime support).

— Most kits come with a parts and labor warranty.

CONS

— Costs more than doing it yourself.

— Takes a little longer to recoup your investment.

— Some processors have many deficiencies. See the Design Checklist on page 110 for things to look for when buying either a ready-to-run processor or a do-it-yourself kit.

— If the seller doesn't describe what safety features they incorporate into their kit, you could end up with a dangerous processor.

— Some ready-to-run processors lack many necessary items, such as safety gear, complete titration kit, scales, and the like. See the section "What Should Come with a Kit or a Ready-to-Run Processor" on page 114 for more information.

— Many processors are poorly designed or leave out extremely important processing instructions and design criteria to achieve high-quality fuel. If you're new to biodiesel, you probably won't know until you've bought and built it. Make sure they incorporate the principles presented in this book, if you want to make high-grade fuel.

— Many biodiesel processors are being marketed. Many kits, however, are put together by people who don't have a thorough understanding of how to make high-quality fuel, or don't know the difference between high-quality fuel and fuel with excess glycerine, monoglycerides, or diglycerides (all of which will cause you problems). Do you want to risk it?

— Some companies cut too many corners, in order to sell the cheapest processor. Remember, if they are cheaper, there's usually a reason. Compare carefully.

Do some research on the company and its history and principal players and designers before buying. Also compare the different processors carefully to make sure they incorporate all the important elements required to make high-quality biodiesel. Finally, since you'll be spending a substantial amount of money, I recommend that you pick a company that sells processors full time, not as a hobby or sideline. Ask about their customer support after the sale, and inquire about their guarantee (for example, is it in writing? how long does it run?).

CHAPTER 6

DESIGNING, BUILDING, OR PURCHASING A PROCESSOR

If you're eager to get going right away, and you don't want the hassle and frustration of designing your own processor, then you're obviously in the market for either a kit or a ready-to-run processor. Since there are several brands out there, how do you know which ones are well designed and which aren't? Here are some guidelines that will help you in your decision-making process. You may even add to this list, based on your needs and circumstances.

DESIGN CHECKLIST

You may need to see our Parts and Materials Guidelines on page 125 for a full explanation of some of the following items.

- ❏ **Parts**—If it's a kit, does it come with *all* the parts you need to put it together?
- ❏ **Processing tank**—Is the processing tank totally draining? If not, you'll have a hard time draining all the glycerine. Then when you drain the biodiesel, some of the glycerine will likely come with it, contaminating the fuel.

Shape of the bottom of a total drain tank. Has no bulkhead fitting.

CONE BOTTOM PROCESSING TANK

- **Supplies**—Does the maker tell you what items or supplies you have to find yourself? Don't assume that any kit is truly "complete." You'll have to buy some items. Your kit supplier should give you a list of what else you'll need, otherwise you may find yourself running down a lot of items you didn't know you'd need.

- **Filters**—Does the processor provide a way to filter the used oil? This is important, for more than the obvious reason. For one, food particles are like little sponges holding onto the water in the oil, which will make soap in your biodiesel. Also, do they provide a way to filter the finished biodiesel?

- **Heat**—Does the design incorporate a way to heat the oil? Some claim that room temperature will do, but one university study showed that heat greatly speeds the reaction up, thereby increasing the total conversion ratio. An incomplete reaction, being invisible, will cause you coking and fouling problems in the long run. You *must* be able to heat the oil in order to make high-quality fuel. And what about making biodiesel during the colder months?

- **Heating method**—How is the oil heated and for how long? Note that some heating elements get far too hot for cooking oil and can actually cause the oil to catch fire.

- **Temperature monitoring**—Is there a way to measure the heat achieved (preferably in the tank)? Measuring outside the tank, in the plumbing, is good only while the pump is running; it doesn't give an idea of heat loss.

- **Temperature regulation**—Is there a way to regulate the temperature—that is, a thermostat? If using a water heater element (as is commonly done), you could easily forget to turn it

55-GALLON BARREL
FILTER

HEATING BARRELS WITH
INSTALLED HEATERS

INFRARED
THERMOMETER
FOR MEASURING
OIL TEMPERATURE

off in time and thereby overheat the oil, possibly starting a fire. This won't happen with the proper heating element plus a thermostat.

❑ **Insulation**—Are the processor and tank lines insulated to reduce heat loss?

❑ **Dewatering**—Does it give you a way to dewater the oil? If you don't remove the water before processing, you could make so much soap that the batch is ruined, so this is an important step.

❑ **Tank venting**—Are the processor and the methoxide mixer both vented safely? They *must* be vented to the outdoors, because venting into the work area is extremely dangerous.

❑ **Processor pump flow**—Is the pump rated at a high-enough flow rate? Pumps that flow at only 330 gph (gallons per hour) are insufficient for anything more than a 20-gallon batch.

❑ **Processor pump mounting**—Is the processor pump mounted properly, both to allow draining the glycerine out of it and to allow easy priming?

❑ **Processor pump priming**—Does the processor have a way to easily prime the pump? Most are nonpriming and need to be primed before use. If it's mounted vertically, you can't prime it using the priming plug on the pump.

❑ **Processor timer**—Does it include a timer that allows you to set times from 1 to 4 hours? You need to be able to adjust your times according to the temperature of the oil. If it cools off due to a phone call or family emergency, you need to be able to run the pump longer.

❑ **Methanol pump**—Does it give you a way to get the methanol from your methanol drum into the methoxide tank (besides pouring it from a 5-gallon can)?

❑ **Methanol mixing**—Does it have a good, *safe* way in its design to mix the lye/methanol, without leaving clumps? It can be difficult to dissolve the catalyst without clumping unless you have the proper design. Does it require you to "manually" mix the methoxide by shaking or rocking a carboy, or a stack of carboys? This is somewhat dangerous, as the carboy could leak or burst. There have been several instances of this happening, spewing methoxide all over.

❑ **Methanol mixer size**—Does the methoxide mixer hold enough methanol for your processor, or do you have to mix up several methoxide batches? We've seen designs that require you to mix several methoxide batches for one batch of oil. This would be very time consuming.

❏ **Methoxide pump**—Does it use an electric pump to mix the methoxide? This might not be the best idea with a flammable fluid such as methanol.

❏ **Methoxide metering**—Does it have a way to meter the methoxide into the processor? Letting it in too fast can result in incomplete mixing and "hot spots" of methoxide.

❏ **Fuel washing**—Does the design include a mist and bubble wash system? Both together work better than a mist washer alone.

❏ **Mister construction**—What is the mister system made out of? (We use one stainless steel misting head.)

❏ **Fuel drying**—Does the design include a way to dry the fuel after washing it (very important)?

❏ **Ball valve material**—Note that PVC stands for polyvinyl chloride (see note about polyvinyl in the Tip box). Does the processor use PVC ball valves? These deteriorate quickly and can even break. Websites have reported many PVC ball valves breaking or seizing up. Since they need to work with a caustic solution and biodiesel, brass or stainless ball valves are much more durable.

❏ **Hoses**—If the processor uses the reinforced clear hoses (which a lot of manufacturers employ), is it thinwall or thickwall? The only hose available at hardware stores is the cheaper thinwall. We've used this, and found that it degrades fairly quickly. We now use heavier gauge hoses that hold up much better, so be sure to ask.

Tip: In its "B100 Material Compatibility" guide, the National Biodiesel Board states that "B100 may degrade some hoses, gaskets, seals, elastomers, glues and plastics with prolonged exposure. Natural or nitrile rubber compounds, polypropylene, *polyvinyl*, and Tygon materials are *particularly vulnerable*." (Emphasis added.)

WHAT SHOULD COME WITH A KIT OR A READY-TO-RUN PROCESSOR

The information in this section applies to both ready-to-run processors and do-it-yourself kits. If you happen to be building your own processor from scratch, however, use this as an equipment and supplies guide.

The question "what should come with a kit?" is a good one to ask, as many "kits" out there conveniently don't bother to mention all the *other* things you will need. If they do mention them, it's a good sign of a more-thorough kit. Most simply don't tell you what you'll have to buy on your own.

Below is a list of many vital things you'll need with *any* processor. If the kit doesn't come with any of these items, this doesn't necessarily mean it's a bad kit—though you should make note of it so you know what else you'll need to buy. You might want to make copies of these checklists, so you can use one for each kit you're considering, making it easier to compare them. Simply check off each item the kit contains, and make notes in the margin.

KIT PARTS AND SUPPLIES CHECKLIST

TYPICAL SAFETY GEAR

1 Safety gear
   - ❏ Goggles or face shield
   - ❏ Respirator (can be simple, but should be of good quality, since the main purpose is to help you avoid breathing KOH or lye particles or dust; respirators *won't* stop methanol fumes)
   - ❏ Gloves (resistant to caustics and methanol)
   - ❏ Apron or labcoat
   - ❏ Safety instructions
2 Titration testing supplies
   - ❏ **Dispensing and measuring apparatus**—Usually a syringe or a pipette (have 3 or more), for measuring and dispensing small amounts of alcohol, oil, and reference solution
   - ❏ **Measuring containers**—Accurately graduated beakers, cylinders, or other ways to measure 5 to 1,000 ml of fluid
   - ❏ Three mixing containers for the titration process (clearly labeled for their intended purpose); best if they have tightly recloseable lids
   - ❏ A way to calculate how much lye and methanol you'll need; either a chart, a formula, or a spreadsheet program (preferred); see the chart on page 220, though it's only for 90 percent KOH, or use the biodiesel calculator listed in the Reference section
   - ❏ Indicator solution (phenolphthalein or turmeric)
   - ❏ Mixing and storage container (for lye/water reference solution) 1 to 2 liter size
   - ❏ Accurate miniscale (accurate to 0.1 g or finer)
3 Larger scale to measure catalyst for larger batches (accurate to 1 g, capacity up to 5+ lbs)
4 Minibatch kit (you need to be able to make test batches before making your first larger batches; even later you'll need the minibatch kit)
5 Accurate, easy-to-understand assembly or setup instructions (should have clear pictures and illustrations, as well as easy-to-understand instructions)
6 Guidebook to understand biodiesel and the process of making it (as in this book)
7 Wiring for the pump (or prewired for ready-to-run processors)
8 Timer switch for the pump (4-hour, to allow for flexibility in processing times)
9 Way to heat the oil, and to control the temperature
10 Insulation for the tank and lines, to minimize heat loss

11 Way to measure the temperature of the oil (preferably in the reactor tank)

12 Mist and bubble washing system

13 Used oil filtration to remove the breading and particles from the used oil

14 Some way to dewater the used cooking oil

15 Some sort of drying system for drying the finished biodiesel

16 A fuel filter to filter the final product

17 Reactor/processing tank (cone bottom tanks drain more thoroughly); make sure the tank can be sealed, to keep methanol fumes from escaping into your work area (stainless would be the best material, but the cost will likely keep that out of most people's price range)

18 Tank stands if needed

19 All valves, fittings, hoses, clamps, and pipes to assemble the kit

20 Mixing pump with a good flow rate of over 500 gph

21 Methoxide mixing method that doesn't involve sparking electrical motors (lye can be hard to dissolve, so you need some type of fairly vigorous mixing)

22 A ventilation system on the methoxide mixing tank, and one on the reactor, that both vent to the outside (not back into your workspace)

23 Heavy-gauge, quality braided lines on the pressurized pumping lines (not just the clear, nonreinforced lines, as they could rupture more easily, spraying dangerous chemicals everywhere)

24 Quality ball valves (PVC valves, even good quality, will seize up and give you problems from the methoxide mixture attacking them); stick with brass ball valves

25 Designed for easy future upgrades so that you can make more biodiesel, faster

26 A guarantee on all parts in the kit

27 A guarantee on the ready-to-run processor parts and labor

28 Free technical support (preferably via phone, a customer website, and e-mail)

PROCESSOR COMPARISONS

When it comes to making biodiesel at home, you have two common safe ways to do this.

Appleseed design—The first way is using an Appleseed-type processor, which basically is one that uses a hot water heater and some external wash tanks. With this design, you heat and process the oil in the water heater, then wash and dry it in separate tanks. A separate carboy container is usually used for mixing the methoxide. This is a popular, do-it-yourself style, because of its fairly simple design and the common availability of water

APPLESEED PROCESSOR (PHOTO COURTESY GRAYDON BLAIR, UTAH BIODIESEL SUPPLY)

heaters. Built properly, this type of processor will make quality fuel.

Cone tank design—The second way to make biodiesel safely involves using two separate polyethylene cone bottom tanks. You'll use one tank to mix the methoxide in, and a second, larger tank to process the biodiesel. The larger tank is typically used for washing the fuel, also. The fuel is dried either externally in separate tanks, or inside the processor itself. This style is also popular owing to its more commercial and clean look, and the fact that you can see the fuel, glycerine,

CONE BOTTOM BIODIESEL PROCESSOR

VERY HOMEMADE PROCESSOR *(THIS STYLE IS NOT RECOMMENDED)*

and water through the semitransparent tank walls. This style of processor, when built properly, will also make high-quality, ASTM-grade fuel.

Some people have built processors from such things as old compressor tanks, propane tanks, 55-gallon drums, and so forth. These all tend to be similar to the Appleseed design, so we'll group them in that category. Then there is the old style of making biodiesel in open-top drums or buckets. **Caution: Never make biodiesel in dangerous, open-top containers like this!** They let the methanol escape into the working area and are extremely dangerous, because of the health hazards of breathing the methanol and the extreme flammability. A simple spark from an electric drill while mixing the biodiesel could ignite it. Please don't build dangerous designs like this in the interest of saving money.

Both of the two safe designs have advantages as well as disadvantages, summarized below. Use this information to help you decide which type of reactor or processor to use.

APPLESEED REACTOR

ADVANTAGES

1   Water heaters are available locally, sometimes free (they usually cost from $300 to $400 when new). The free ones are often full of water deposits and sediments that preferably should first be cleaned out. Some may be so full of deposits that you can't get them clean. Leaving all that crud behind could ruin your biodiesel-making efforts.
2   The water tank is made from a heavy-gauge steel, making it extremely durable.
3   Steel tanks are highly resistant to chemicals.
4   A built-in heater can make it easy for you to preheat your oil, but it can't heat thick, cold oil *before* it can be pumped into the tank. (You may need a separate barrel heater.)
5   Can be made mostly fumeless.
6   Doesn't require welding, unlike processors made from steel barrels or from scratch.
7   Popular "do-it-yourself" style.
8   Free instructions are often available on the Internet.
9   Plans are available at reasonable cost.

1   You can't see into the tank while processing. This can leave you
    wondering what's happening. Also, you can't view problems like
    glop, soaps, and so on. Nor can you see liquid draining and
    levels, except in the sight glass.

2   Very hard to clean out if you make glop.

3   Doesn't have the steep, conical bottom of a cone bottom tank,
    which makes draining and separation harder. You could more
    easily end up with leftover glycerine in your tank, which can
    contaminate your fuel.

4   May still require a separate heater to preheat the oil to make it
    pumpable in winter.

5   Tank sizes are somewhat limited. Poly tanks come in all sizes.

6   Preparing the water heater for use as a processor can be
    daunting for some. Many people find it difficult to locate parts
    on the tank, such as the anode, breather tube, pressure vent, and
    upper element.

7   Still uses some plastic (hoses, hose fittings); almost all
    processors do.

8   Can be difficult to find easy-to-understand free designs (ones for
    sale may be more detailed).

9   Can require more skill to build than you may possess.

10 Requires separate mist/bubble washing tank, adding to the
    space required.

11 Looks a little less professional and clean in design than a cone
    bottom design. Many people dislike the homemade, pieced-
    together look of this design. Some designs are sleeker than
    others, so check around. This may be a factor with your spouse
    or neighbor.

12 Methoxide mixing is usually done 5 gallons at a time, by rocking
    a carboy for 30 minutes. This can require you to swap out several
    carboys in the middle of a mixing run if you're making more
    than about 15 gallons.

13 Mixing methoxide in a carboy is cheap, but can be dangerous, as
    many carboys have sprung a leak, spewing caustic methoxide
    all over.

14 Adding the methanol to the carboy requires opening the small
    lid and pouring, pumping, or siphoning it in. Cone bottom tanks
    can be pumped into without allowing vapors into the work area.

15 If you accidentally turn the heating element on while the processor has the biodiesel or oil/methoxide mixture in it, you risk igniting the methanol. Homebrewers discussing this event on the Internet have had this happen, as there's no safety lock to prevent it.

16 Washing is often done in open-top barrels. Since methanol remains in the biodiesel at this point, there's a possibility of methanol getting into your workspace.

CONE BOTTOM MDPE (MEDIUM-DENSITY POLYETHYLENE) PROCESSOR

ADVANTAGES

1 Semiclear plastic enables you to easily see the level of fluids in the tank without opening the lid.

2 You can look in the top and see the biodiesel mixture brewing and what it looks like. (For beginners, this is easier than a sight tube.) Most people like being able to see things happening. Even after making hundreds of batches, I still enjoy looking in and seeing that everything is flowing well.

3 Conical bottom allows for more complete biodiesel/glycerine separation than flat-bottom wash tanks. By funneling all the fluid down to a point, the interface layer between the glycerine and the biodiesel is much shallower, which allows a more thorough—and accurate—draining of the glycerine, or water.

4 Able to achieve a total drain of the glycerine, leaving none behind to contaminate your fuel. This is due to the cone shape and the new total-drain designs.

5 Able to do your mist and bubble washing in the same tank.

6 Doesn't require welding.

7 Tank is easy to drill through when installing a water wash or other device.

8 Uses a lightweight tank.

9 Polyethylene tanks are highly resistant to chemicals.

10 Commercial grade polyethylene tanks are

CONE BOTTOM TANKS ALLOW YOU TO SEE THE LEVEL OF FLUIDS

extremely durable. It would take something on the order of a
forklift hitting one to damage it.

11 Doesn't require you to first disassemble a water heater before
you can build the processor.

12 Easier to clean out if you make a glop batch, since you can
remove the lid.

13 Professional, clean-looking design.

14 By using a barrel heater to preheat the oil, you need only one oil
heater.

15 Enables you to use the barrel heater to dewater the oil. All used
cooking oil has water in it, and by heating it in the separate
heating barrel you can settle the watery oil to the bottom and
avoid it. This allows you to preheat the oil and dewater in the
same barrel, at the same time. Also removes the possibility of
igniting the methanol, as in an Appleseed design.

16 Methoxide mixers can be built to mix all the methoxide at once, in
a safe cone bottom tank, requiring no manual shaking or mixing
and only one mixing tank (as opposed to numerous carboys).

17 Methanol can be pumped into the tank with the lid closed,
reducing the escaping methanol vapors to nearly zero.

18 Methanol tank can be securely mounted to the floor, reducing
the likelihood of accidental spills. Carboys in an Appleseed must
be handled carefully to avoid accidental spills.

19 With a sealed lid, plus a vent tube attached to a hose leading to
the outside, you can make this system mostly fumeless, like the
Appleseed.

20 It's possible to make a spark-free mixing system for the
methoxide tank, which is semiautomated.

DRAWBACKS

1 MDPE cone bottom tanks are only rated to 140°F, which would
be a problem only if you seriously overheated the oil, since
quality fuel should be made at temperatures of 120° to 130°F.
Methanol starts evaporating at 148°F, so you should never
approach that temperature. Never put a heating element in an
MDPE tank, and never add oil that's over 145°F (it'll cool about
10 to 15 degrees when added to a cool tank), then you'll be fine.
Thousands of individuals and businesses use a cone bottom
MDPE tank, with no heat-related problems.

2 There are no known "free" instruction plans for this type of
reactor.

3   Can require more skill than you have if you decide to build it yourself from scratch.

4   Not able to heat inside the tank with a direct heating element. If you really wanted to, though, you could heat in the tank with a heat transfer system that pumps a hot fluid through tubes in the tank.

5   Not quite as durable as a metal hot water heater tank. This is a problem only if you hit it with a vehicle or something. You'll never damage one under normal use.

6   Not likely to find free poly tanks (unlike free hot water heaters).

OTHER CONSIDERATIONS

If you've read on the Internet about biodiesel processors, you may have been convinced how much safer the Appleseed is. Personally, I believe that both it and the cone bottom processor are safe if designed and used properly.

The primary reason some state the danger of poly tanks is that they can't withstand a fire, and any fuel that might be in them could catch fire, adding to the fire's intensity. Let me explain that rationale a little bit.

First, the only time biodiesel is in the processor is when you're making it. Once biodiesel has been processed in either the Appleseed or the cone bottom style, it's transferred out to poly washing tanks (essentially, 55-gallon poly drums with one end cut out). After washing is complete, most people store their finished biodiesel in a poly tank anyway, no matter what they made it in. So with the Appleseed style, the only time it's in a steel tank is when processing. After that, most of us store our biodiesel in poly tanks, which makes the steel tank's safety a moot point

Second, I've yet to read of a fire starting in a processor of any type. If used safely, either style should be as safe as the other.

Third, the drum of methanol concerns me much more than the biodiesel itself. Biodiesel has a flash point twice that of petrodiesel, which basically means it has to get extremely hot to ignite. You can't ignite biodiesel even with a brief pass of a torch. (Believe me, I've tried!) Therefore, biodiesel itself is as safe a fuel as we have, even in the event of a fire.

BUILDING YOUR OWN PROCESSOR

If you've read everything above and still want to build your own processor, here are some pointers. I won't go into detail about exactly how to build a processor, since there are several ways to do that—and that's a separate book in itself. But I *will* give you some pointers and tips, along with Internet links taking you to websites offering free plans for the Appleseed and to sites containing some good, professionally drawn plans for the Appleseed. The latter plans cost a little, but are well done.

First, you have to decide what type of processor you want. That's what the above section should have helped you with. As described above, processors fall into basically two types: the Appleseed processor and the cone bottom MDPE processor.

If you decide to build the Appleseed type reactor, you can find plans to do that on the Internet, for free (see website list below). That's the big advantage with this design. Yet the plans differ from one author/designer to the next, and some are better written than others. So you might have to read over several pages of plans, and then splice them all together to build the one you want. This could take some time. Or you can save time and simply buy kits containing instructions and/or parts.

If you decide to build the cone bottom MDPE reactor from free plans, good luck with that…as I haven't found any free instructions on how to build one. You could probably spend a month or so and come up with a design that will work for you, and then build it—or you can simply buy a kit, or a ready-to-run processor.

WEBSITES TO FIND MORE INFORMATION ON THE APPLESEED

www.Biodieselcommunity.org/appleseedprocessor
Contains free plans and pictures of the original Appleseed.

www.ezbiodiesel.com/bookbonus.htm
We are an authorized distributor for the most professionally drawn and illustrated Appleseed kit available—from Utah Biodiesel, one of the best Appleseed style vendors out there. Its plans are all computer rendered, with thorough illustrations and instructions.

This company has the best Appleseed kit I've seen, and the staff is great to work with.

The illustration below is an example of the quality drawings in its kit.

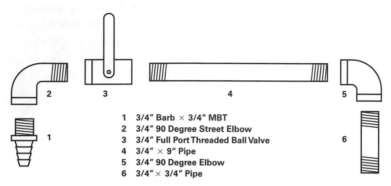

1   3/4" Barb × 3/4" MBT
2   3/4" 90 Degree Street Elbow
3   3/4" Full Port Threaded Ball Valve
4   3/4" × 9" Pipe
5   3/4" 90 Degree Elbow
6   3/4" × 3/4" Pipe

SAMPLE OF THE PLANS IN THE APPLESEED KIT ON AUTHOR'S WEBSITE

CONE BOTTOM MDPE PROCESSORS

The only kits we know of for this style can be found at *www. biodieselkitsonline.com*, so I will describe these kit options.

Option 1: Kits—This is the best option for the person who wants to do all the work but not spend forever chasing down all the parts. The kit will include all the instructions and parts needed to completely assemble your own professional biodiesel processor. You will be told exactly what you'll have to supply (which is very little, as the kit even includes the tanks and stands). These kits are thoroughly illustrated with full color as well as black-and-white photos. Most parts are preassembled, saving you even more time, as you then only have to install the sections through the tank. At present this website is the only one offering do-it-yourself kits for the cone bottom processors.

Option 2: Ready-to-Run Processors—You can also find a wide selection of ready-to-run biodiesel processors on the Internet. You can find models for making 20 gallons or several thousand gallons. Some companies such as ours will also custom design larger systems to meet your needs. Most ready-to-run processors come fully assembled ready to begin making biodiesel. With less than 30 minutes' setup time (for some brands), you'll be set to begin making high-quality, washed and dried biodiesel (provided that they include a wash and dry system with their processors). Our EZbiodiesel

ANOTHER STYLE OF CONE BOTTOM, READY-TO-RUN PROCESSOR

brand of processors are among the few ready-to-run processors that incorporate all the important design principles without taking shortcuts. You may find others with enough research. Just be sure to fully research all you find, to make sure that you're getting a complete system, with the proper design, instructions, and support. When we first looked at biodiesel processors, we found that many brands leave out numerous things you'll need to make biodiesel. That leaves you to figure them out on your own and chase these items down. If you want to get started quickly, check out our line of processors and kits at *www.ezbiodiesel.com/bookbonus.htm*. (*Note:* You'll find a coupon on that webpage for our book customers only, giving them an additional $50 off any processor or kit.)

No matter what choice you make, keep in mind the items named in the design checklist at the beginning of this chapter. If you pay attention to those items, and your responses, you can design or purchase a kit that will make high-quality fuel.

PARTS AND MATERIALS GUIDELINES

For the parts you use to build your own, or when buying a ready-to-run processor, here are a few guidelines to observe.

Tanks—Of course, the ultimate material for tanks is stainless steel. If you can afford this, it will outlast all other materials and give the best performance. But it is very pricey, so expect to pay about 10 to 20 times as much for a stainless tank. The next choice is MDPE (medium density polyethylene),

TYPICAL POLY TANK

which makes a very chemically resistant, extremely durable tank. These will hold up very well for homebrew biodiesel use. Another choice is a water heater tank, which typically is made of plain steel, though occasionally you'll find a galvanized one. Do not use the galvanized tanks, as galvanized parts react negatively with biodiesel. As noted earlier, some people have courted disaster by making their processors from salvage items like old compressor tanks or steel drums. Be supercareful when using these, as many old tanks are in poor shape, contain explosive fumes, or are not sealable. And you do not want to use tanks that cannot be sealed, as you'll release toxic and flammable methanol vapors into your workspace.

Fittings—For valves, use brass valves, which work well and are affordable. For fittings, use malleable black iron, not galvanized (which may have an undesired chemical reaction with the biodiesel).

Ball Valves—Brass valves are the most commonly used valve and are acceptable, as is steel. Even though I say later that brass should be avoided, that caution applies primarily to commercial producers. Most brass valves also contain a chromed or stainless ball with a Teflon seat. So the only part actually in contact with the biodiesel is where the pipe threads into it, a quite small area. PVC ball valves should be avoided (see below), as they have a bad reputation for not holding up well, and many have broken. This is likely due to the corrosiveness of the methoxide, plus the biodiesel and even the cooking oil. We have used PVC ball valves on several areas of our oil collection setup, and even these try to seize up. We end up having to use pliers to break them free, eventually breaking the valve.

Hoses and Plumbing—Most homebrew processors use flexible, reinforced PVC hose that runs from the mixing pump to the processor tank. This is popular because the hose allows you to see the fluids flowing through them, acting as a sight glass. Although PVC is not a highly recommended material, if you purchase the thickwall hoses they'll hold up well, since they usually contain

REINFORCED TRANSPARENT PVC HOSE

fluids for relatively short periods. Still, these hoses have two disadvantages. First, they degrade in time, due to the heat and chemicals. With simple monitoring, though, you'll know when it's time to replace them (a simple process). Heavy-wall hoses last about twice as long as the big-box store type hoses. The second disadvantage is that PVC hoses tend to weep slightly. This doesn't actually hurt anything, but the hoses will almost always have a light sheen of biodiesel on them. We just wipe them off occasionally so that they don't collect dust.

Tip: Never use nonreinforced hose in your processor, as it can easily rupture and spew caustic methoxide or hot oil all over the place. Always use heavy-wall, reinforced hose on any pressurized or suction side of your processor.

Other Parts—Natural or nitrile rubber compounds, polypropylene, polyvinyl, and Tygon-brand materials are particularly vulnerable. PVC falls into the polyvinyl class above, although hoses that have plasticizers in them seem to hold up fairly well. Brass, bronze, copper, lead, tin, and zinc all may accelerate the oxidation process of biodiesel, creating fuel insolubles or gels and salts. Galvanized metal should be avoided, as should copper pipes, brass regulators, and copper fittings; if used in small amounts, these won't greatly affect the small-scale homebrewer, and are of more concern to commercial producers and those who store fuel for longer periods. When assembling the processor, you can use plumbers pipe dope, which can be messy, or Teflon tape. Such tape comes in white or yellow; the latter is a bit better because it's thicker, usually meets mil specs, goes farther, and seals better, but is more expensive.

Oil Heater—Whatever type of system you build, be sure to incorporate some method of heating the oil to about 130° or 140°F before you add the methoxide. But DON'T heat it once the methoxide is added, for safety's sake. And don't heat above 148°F or you'll boil away the methanol. Probably the safest method is to use a drum band heater, which is thermostatically controlled and can be plugged directly into a wall outlet. They can be a little slow to heat, so if you need a faster method you can stack two or three heaters on a barrel. Or see the section on building a barrel heater (page 142) for a simple solution made from common parts. Any kit or processor you buy should come with an oil heater.

Pump and Mixer—Most people use an inexpensive Harbor Freight brand clearwater pump for their processors. Such a pump will work, though the flow rate is far too slow. A better choice is Northern Industrial's pump, which looks similar but flows twice as fast. Our kits incorporate this pump with double the flow rate of the

PROCESSOR PUMP

Harbor Freight pump; this ensures more thorough mixing, faster fuel transfer, and easier priming.

If you purchase your pump elsewhere, look for one with a flow rate of 10 gpm or higher so that you can process up to 80 gallons per batch. And look for a pump that's called a TEFC (totally enclosed, fan-cooled) pump, which is less inclined to spark, since all the motor's electrical parts are sealed in a fully enclosed housing. Be aware that, unless it's rated "Explosion Proof," there's still a very small chance of an explosion if you have a lot of methanol fumes in the area. You might also look for a pump that's rated for higher temperature fluids, as well as mild to medium corrosiveness. The pump we mentioned seems to hold up very well for this process, and is very affordable. The price for a better pump like this is about 10 times that of the cheaper pump. For safety, it's always best to mix the methoxide *away from* any electrical pumps.

Methoxide Mixer—If you decide to use the carboy methoxide mixing method, instructions for that can be found on the same website as the information for the Appleseed reactor. You basically take 2 carboys, put a fitting in the lids (which allows you to hook up about a ½" vinyl hose), and plumb that to your processor. To mix in these, you simply add the methanol and lye and then rock the containers a few times, about 5 to 10 minutes apart, over the course of about 30 to 45 minutes. Do this until you can no longer see lye particles in the bottom of the carboy.

Drawbacks are the time you have to spend rocking the carboys, and the hassle of changing carboys in the middle of a batch (when making batches of larger than 20 gallons).

If you'll be making a cone bottom methoxide mixer, there are a few things to consider:

— Whenever the tank contains methanol, you'll want to minimize the time that the lid is open on the processor. The best way to do this is to design it so that you can just pump the methanol into the tank through hoses, PVC pipe, and the like. Since you can see the level, you won't need to open the tank to know when you have enough in it.

— If you can funnel in the catalyst, that's even better. Look for a funnel with as large an outlet as possible. The best kind is what's called a "powder funnel," which has parallel sides on the output spout that help avoid powder compaction (which will clog the funnel).

— You need a way to stir the methanol. An air-driven pump will work well if you pump from the bottom and back into the top, or vice versa, though this type is a bit expensive when new (you might find one used for a good deal less money). The ideal pump is air powered, groundable, and explosion proof. Or, buy an electric, explosion-proof pump. Short of all that, use the same pump as on the processor, since it will be a TEFC pump (see page 128). This way, all the sparking components are sealed inside the pump, and the pump is cooled by cooling fins. Note that while the electrical parts are fairly well sealed, this type of pump is technically NOT explosion proof; to be rated as such requires rigorous testing and certification, so if you use this type, do so at your own discretion.

— When adding the catalyst, you should add it after the methanol. Add it over a 15-second or longer period, to avoid having the mixture start "boiling" and bubbling, which can splash the caustic solution all over you. Even adding it slowly can clog the bottom of either the cone bottom tank or the pump. One way to avoid this is to buy a simple, stainless steel, sink strainer and attach it to the bulkhead fitting upside down. This will help, but you may have to devise another method to keep the catalyst from clumping up at the bottom.

— Your methoxide mixer needs a one-way check valve on the output so that the fluid will flow out only. Otherwise, if you forget and leave the valves open, the biodiesel can flow back into the methoxide tank once the pump shuts off. Cleaning the biodiesel and glycerine out of the tank can be messy.

— You can control how fast the methoxide goes into the biodiesel processor by using a ball valve on the output.

— Plumb the output of this tank into the suction side of the processor pump, so that it can draw the output into the oil via suction *only*.

— If you use a ⅜" line on the processor, a ⅜" to ½" line is big enough on the methoxide tank.

Electrical—To avoid shorts, fires, or overheating the pump or heating element, be sure to use the appropriate size and type of wiring on your system. If your system has any switches at all, you should put them in enclosed exterior electrical boxes to prevent any possible methanol vapors from getting into the box where a spark could occur. I suggest putting the heating element on a separate circuit in your service panel, along with its own breaker. That way you can turn it on and off remotely, and with ease. If you are not an electrician, please be safe and hire one for all your electrical chores. It can be extremely dangerous to do your own wiring unless you know exactly what you're doing. One idea: Trade the labor for some biodiesel, since many electricians drive diesel trucks.

Mister and Bubble Washer—All you need here is a good aquarium air pump rated for approximately the number of gallons of biodiesel you'll be making, some aquarium air hose, a misting system, and an air stone (a limewood air bubbler works well, but you'll need to weight it down to make it sink). *Note:* Don't buy an actual air stone, which won't hold up in your system. And never put anything with cheap plastic on it in your biodiesel, because the fuel will melt the plastic (it's happened to me). If you buy the right mister, you can get by with just one

SINGLE HEAD MISTING NOZZLE

misting head instead of having to use the five or six misters that formerly were typically used. Reason: One mister is simpler and clogs much less. Just plumb the misters above your washing tank, and you're ready to mist. Then when you're set to bubble wash, drop the air stone in the bottom and turn on the air pump.

Safety Tip: All washing should be done with the tank sealed, because residual methanol will be in the biodiesel until you finish washing.

Biodiesel Dryer—To dry the biodiesel after washing it, you can simply leave it in an open-top barrel for several days to a week or more. It will eventually dry this way unless you're in a very humid or cold climate. Or, to dry it much faster you can use a dedicated drying device to dry the fuel. To do this, use an open-top 55-gallon drum and a fan to air dry it. If you can find a way to pump the fuel in a circulation mode into and out of the tank, and can make the

fuel "fan" out, it will dry faster. See the "spray drying example" photo
on this page. Anything that will spread the fuel out to increase the
surface area will help. It works this way: Use a pump to recirculate
the biodiesel in and out of the open-top barrel (often the processor
pump doubles as the drying pump), and as it sprays back into the
tank you spray it out in a fan shape. If you have an actual fan
blowing toward the drying area, the drying action will be speeded
up, because the moving air will carry more moisture away faster.
The fuel will usually dry in 1½ to 4 hours this way. If you use the
processor pump, you can also use its timer to control the drying
time.

In high-humidity areas or on colder days, you might want to use
a 300-watt aquarium heater, which will heat the biodiesel to 90°F. If
you do this, *be careful*, as the heater can melt through a plastic
drum. Just suspend it in the middle and you should be fine.

Or you can build a more sophisticated, and more expensive, flash
evaporation unit, which works like this: The biodiesel is heated to

SPRAY DRYING EXAMPLE

about 220°F in a pressurized
container. The pressure raises
the boiling point of the water
so it's very hot but not boiling.
Then the fuel is sent to a
second chamber where it's
sprayed into a cool chamber
under vacuum. Once the hot
biodiesel enters the nonpres-
surized chamber, it instantly
"flashes" the water to steam,
which is drawn out by the
vacuum pump while the
biodiesel falls to the bottom
and is drawn out that way.
This method is instantaneous,
but it requires more energy
and greater capital outlay.

BIODIESEL DRYING BARRELS IN USE

Our EZBiodiesel brand
processors use a proprietary,
but simple, air evaporation
system. This dries the fuel in
about two hours, using very

little electricity. The process is similar to taking a gallon can of lacquer thinner and taking the lid off to let it evaporate. It will, but

it'll probably take about a week. If you pour the lacquer thinner out on concrete in a light breeze, it'll evaporate *much* more quickly. That's basically how our method works.

Biodiesel Filtration—You should incorporate a filtration system into the final output of your biodiesel pump. Almost any diesel fuel filter of around 5 to 10 microns will work fine. Put the filter on the final output where you pump the biodiesel to your car, gas can, or storage container.

BIODIESEL FILLING STATION WITH FUEL FILTER ATTACHED

MAKING BIODIESEL IN LARGE BATCHES

To make high-quality biodiesel, you must follow several guidelines that are *extremely* important to the process. If you leave out any of these points, you may end up with substandard fuel that could result in failed batches or even damage to your engine. *We didn't just make up these guidelines, and we didn't just fall off a turnip truck.* They come directly from the University of Idaho's guidelines for homebrewers, and we follow them almost to the letter. For those who don't know, that university's biodiesel education and fuels research program has pioneered many advancements in biodiesel, and it is considered the most knowledgeable source for biodiesel on both large and small scales.

Here is an actual excerpt from that report, and these are the critical points from that report (a link to the full report is in the back of the book, and on our website):

"A frequent mistake of homebrewers is to add too little methanol or not allow sufficient time. Reports of as little as 13 to 15% methanol (compared with the 22% recommended here) are heard frequently. This is unlikely to produce a good-quality biodiesel. Although it can be difficult for homebrewers to confirm that their product meets the specifications of the ASTM standard, this is a goal that we recommend they strive to achieve. In addition to adding enough alcohol, it is important for homebrewers to provide enough agitation, enough temperature, and enough time for the reaction to reach completion. We recommend that the reaction be allowed 1–2 hours at 140°F, 2–4 hours at 105°F, or 4–8 hours at 70°F. We recommend that the oil, alcohol, and catalyst be stirred vigorously throughout the reaction period."

Many manufacturers fail to include all the steps that are required. So make sure any processor you buy satisfies *all* the following requirements and processes:

— Selection of the better oils
— Dewatering (in two steps)
— Heating to the proper temperature
— Accurate titrations and measurements
— Correct agitation time and method
— Proper pump size, to ensure that mixture stays mixed
— Thorough washing
— Drying the finished biodiesel
— Settling
— Not rushing the process
— Giving everything plenty of time to work, so that you'll end up with higher quality fuel

PROCESS OF MAKING LARGE BATCHES OF BIODIESEL

I'll break down the process of making a large batch of biodiesel in three sections.

First, I will name each and every step that you'll take when making a larger batch of biodiesel (say, more than 10 gallons). I'll do that first in a "Simplified List" on the next page.

Second, I'll explain each step of the process in the "Full Explanations" section below.

Third, I'll give you a short overview of the titration and one of the processing instructions, which you can copy and post in your work area. These will be titled the "Titration Quick Reference Guide" (on page 165) and the "Processing Instructions Overview" sheet (on page 166). Use the quick reference guides when titrating the oil, or making the biodiesel, but if you have a question about any of the steps, refer to the detailed explanations below.

SIMPLIFIED LIST

Do these in the exact order listed.

1 Selecting the oil
2 Prefiltering
3 Dewatering
4 Heating the oil
5 Transferring the oil to the processor
6 Doing a titration on the oil
7 Mixing the catalyst and methanol together
8 Transferring the methoxide to the processor
9 Agitating and mixing the methoxide and oil
10 Settling
11 Draining the glycerine
12 Water washing
13 Dry washing (optional, in place of water washing, or in addition to it)
14 Drying the washed fuel
15 Final settling
16 Final filtering

FULL EXPLANATIONS

SELECTING THE OIL

While biodiesel can be made from virtually any form of vegetable oil, yellow grease, brown grease, animal fat, tallow, or lard, I recommend that you be selective in the oil you choose to process. The main reason is that oil that's quite high in FFAs, water, tallow, or other substances can be *very difficult* to process in a homebrew biodiesel processor. Even if you happen to succeed once in making biodiesel with poor-quality oil by using the single-stage process and transesterification, the biodiesel that results will be of poor quality, full of monoglycerides and diglycerides. Therefore, the best idea by far is to select the best oil—and leave the rest.

Oil that thickens or solidifies at high temperatures will also gel up at those same temperatures. Some feedstocks are thus not suitable for processing in areas of the country that have cold weather (though they may be usable in the warmer months).

Before taking it home, test your new oil source, as described in Chapter 2. Ask your source (typically a restaurant) how often they change it, and also whether they leave the lid off their barrels, dump water or trash into it, or contaminate it with other things. Note that merely looking in their oil barrel may be deceptive, as the good oil will usually rise to the top and the really bad gunk will be down at the bottom. I sometimes take a stick and poke down to the bottom to feel how thick the gunk layer is. Sometimes it's 60 percent or more gunk. For the best oil, look for oil that titrates at 3 ml or less. Up to 5 ml is usable, but may leave behind monoglycerides and diglycerides, and over 5 ml is actually out of the range of a single-stage transesterification.

PREFILTERING

The prefiltering step removes large debris from the oil, such as breading and food chunks, before you process it into biodiesel. The large debris is like a sponge and holds a lot of water. By removing this debris, you are removing many of the potential water problems.

Unlike filtering for straight vegetable oil use (SVO) use, you really don't need to filter it that finely. The fine contaminants will settle out in the glycerol layer when you add the methoxide.

You can prefilter your waste cooking oil in several ways. I'll list five of the better, simpler ideas:

— Supply the restaurant a barrel with a built-in coarse filter. You can buy one on the Internet, or make one to fit your barrel out of something like the expanded metal shown in the photo. You can buy the metal screen at some hardware stores or a metal supply company. Make sure it's not too fine or it will clog quickly, which will upset the restaurant manager. I use about a ¼" to ½" opening on ours. If you make it so that it can be locked on, this also stops others from pumping oil out of our barrels. The restaurant has to clean the debris off the filter every now and then, but they usually don't mind. They can just put it into a box and throw it into their dumpster, which saves us from bringing a lot of debris home.

EXPANDED METAL CAN BE USED TO ROUGH FILTER YOUR WVO

— Pump the oil through a window screen placed on top of your preheating barrel. This simple method works well. The easy way to do this is to lay the screen over the barrel, making it sag so the oil runs to the middle and not the edges. Then put the lid ring back on, which will hold the screen in place. Not the slickest method, but it works.

55-GALLON BARREL FILTER

— Buy a 55-gallon barrel filter (available at *www.USPlastics.com*). These fit nicely into your drum and come in fine medium and coarse. Coarse (600 micron) is the best choice, as it doesn't clog up as often and is similar in coarseness to a window screen.

We've found another simple method that involves a mesh, office-style "trash can" that's simply hung inside the barrel. The oil is pumped through this, and because it's deep, and steel mesh from top to bottom, it can filter out a lot of debris before it clogs. If it starts getting full, we simply take it out and empty it. This can also work in the barrel you leave at the restaurant. Hang it slightly lower than the top of the barrel, in case it

STEEL MESH TRASH CAN, USED TO FILTER WVO

does overflow, then it won't overflow the sides of the barrel, ending up on the floor (another "been there/done that!" story).

Use a bag filter. These are simply cloth bags of varying fineness that will filter the oil. If you go this route, get a coarse filter, to avoid constant clogging. If you can afford the housing that it goes in as well, you can pump the oil directly through this before it gets to your heating barrel or processor. Otherwise you'll have to hang it inside the barrel and pump the oil through it that way.

DEWATERING

This step involves removing the majority of the water that's in your oil, *before* processing it. It's extremely important that you remove as much water as you can from your oil, to avoid making excess soap and possible failed batches. If you make too much soap, you'll have a much harder time washing it, because the soap and leftover methanol will work to hold the wash water in suspension. If there's excess soap, it will hold a corresponding lot of water in suspension, and you could end up with an emulsion that's very time consuming to break. At some point the excess water can actually produce a runaway chain reaction that ends up making so *much* soap that the batch fails and ends up as glop or unusable fuel.

Note: The methods described below work best if the oil has been prefiltered, because the chunks of breading and such in the oil hold a lot of water.

Here are the three common ways to remove water from the oil before processing it.

HEAT AND LET SETTLE

A good way to deal with water in your oil is to heat the oil to about 165°F. (See "Heating the Oil" below.) Once at that temperature, the oil is thinned down, and since the water is heavier than the oil it will settle to the bottom. Let it settle overnight and then don't use the bottom 3 to 6 inches or so, as this is where the watery oil will be. You usually won't see a distinct layer of water but will get a watery, murky oil at the bottom instead.

This method works best if the tank in which you heat the oil is insulated and in a warm room. (See the section on building a drum oil preheater on page 142 for important guidelines.) The longer the oil stays warm, the better the water will settle out. But if you use a heating element instead of a band heater, you'll notice that when

the element is on, the oil actually rolls or roils, due to a strong convection current. So if you try leaving the heating element on all night, each time it turns back on, the convection currents could restir the water back into the oil. Therefore, instead, just heat it up, turn it off, and let it settle. You can use a spring-wound timer here also, if you keep your element at 1500W or less. Or use a band heater low on the barrel, as it will have a built-in thermostat.

SPRING-WOUND
TIMER

BOIL IT AWAY

Another way to dry the oil is to boil the water away at about 250°F until it stops boiling. Boiling the oil to get rid of water can be expensive and take a long time, even with a 240V heater element. And it's *extremely* difficult with a 120V element. (See "Heating the Oil" below.) You should never use an open flame beneath an oil barrel, because the oil can form steam pockets and erupt over the barrel sides, catching on fire, and...well, you get the point. Oil *will* catch on fire fairly easily when it spills on an open fire, so avoid open flames.

LONG-TERM SETTLING

If you're building up a surplus stock of oil, you may be able to use this method. It's simplicity itself: Let the oil settle for several weeks before you use it—no fuss, no muss. By letting it settle, the heavier gunk settles to the bottom of your tank. Then you just drain that away and use the rest, or pump off the top and leave the bottom in the tank.

You might want to test the oil you pump off to see how effective it was for you, since the oil temperature, air temperature, type of oil, and time spent settling will all affect the overall results. This works best if you prefilter the oil, which takes out large chunks of breading and similar matter that hold water in suspension. It also works best in cone bottom tanks as the cone shape focuses the gunk to a small area, allowing more complete removal of the gunk layer. This works better in warm regions or during warmer times of the year, which is why a solar preheater setup can help here. (See the section on solar preheating in Chapter 2, page 69.)

Of course, if you're creative, you may come up with other ways to heat the oil. Two methods I've heard about are heating the oil under

CONE BOTTOM TANKS USED FOR LONG-TERM SETTLING

a compost pile (which heats up to about 160°F on its own), and incorporating a passive solar water heating system to circulate hot water (heated by the compost) in coils that pass through the oil. (If you build a waste oil heater (see Resources for details), you could possibly circulate water over the heater and pass it back through the oil in coils.) The possibilities are limited only by your resourcefulness.

Or, you can just use the oil as is and hope for the best. Some brewers have found that wet oil that's low in FFAs is fairly forgiving of water content. Still, it's best to find oil that's as low in water content as possible. Generally, watery oil is also higher in FFAs; this may indicate excessive oil use before changing, though that's not always the case. For example, if rainwater has gotten into the barrel, there might not be an actual FFA problem. Rainwater that gets into restaurant oil barrels tends to settle more easily than water from the food fryers.

HEATING THE OIL

There's some misinformation out in the field regarding the need for heat during the biodiesel-making process. Yes, you can make biodiesel at room temperature, but you're more likely to end up with low-grade fuel containing many monoglycerides and diglycerides. Heat helps the proper reaction take place.

The fact is, heat is extremely important. According to a study done at Iowa State University,[65] to achieve a 0.15 percent total glycerol requirement at 80°F took 4½ hours. By contrast, heating the reaction to only 100°F drove the time required back to less than 2 hours. Heating to 120°F achieved the same result in less than 45 minutes. The study's author concluded that the chance of reaching complete reaction at the lower temperatures was marginal at best. Keep in mind that ASTM standards allow a 0.24 percent total glycerine level; the university study was shooting for slightly better quality than the standards dictate.

Bottom line: To achieve a complete reaction, you need to heat the oil to about 120° to 130°F and try to keep it there during the entire reaction process. (You may want to start at a bit higher temperature if your oil temperature drops as you're adding it to your processor or while you're mixing the methanol, for example.) When you start adding the methoxide, the oil should reach at least 110°F but no more than 135°F. If the temperature drops 10°F or so during the entire process, I wouldn't worry about it. (That's one reason to always run the pump about 20 percent longer than needed, strictly as a safety measure.) Not maintaining enough heat or agitation time can result in additional monoglycerides and diglycerides, both of which are invisible and can cause problems. Running way too long—such as in three extra hours—may result in excess soap formation, so avoid that as well. An extra hour is fine. (See the troubleshooting hints in Chapter 10 for more ideas.)

Tip: Methanol boils at 148°F, so avoid getting the mixture too hot or you'll boil off most of the methanol, or even all of it.

Another good idea is to insulate your processors tank and lines well, to ensure that you hold the heat in for as long as possible. We've found that the foil/bubble/foil type insulation such as the Reflectix brand (sold at places like big-box home improvement stores) works well for insulating the heating barrels. Our brand of biodiesel processors use this same type of insulation, but we have a proprietary brand that's rated at about 1.5 to 2 times the insulation value of the big-box brand.

HEATING IN AN APPLESEED REACTOR

You can heat your oil in the tank with an Appleseed reactor, though in the winter you may need to preheat it to even pump it into the tank in the first place. Even if you have an Appleseed reactor with a built-in heating element, it's not recommended that you turn the element on once you've added the methoxide. Doing so can be dangerous due to hot steam pockets forming under the glycerol, thus overheating the oil and possibly causing a fire from too much heat. Cases have also been documented of methanol explosions in these tanks from turning the heater on when methanol fumes were present in the tank. Luckily, no one has yet been hurt by this. Others have used the heating element to "break" an emulsion. This is still dangerous due to the methanol that still remains in the biodiesel at that point. Bottom line: Avoid turning on a heating element in the oil or biodiesel if there may be methanol in it.

WAYS TO HEAT THE OIL

BUILD A 55-GALLON DRUM PREHEATER

DRUM HEATERS

If you want a way to preheat your oil *before* it goes into your processor, or a way to dewater your oil, consider using a homemade drum heater. First off, this involves electrical wiring, so **I STRONGLY SUGGEST that you hire an electrician to hook this up for you—to be entirely safe.** *Disclaimer: We are providing the following details for Information Only.*

This is for the barrel preheater. With a 110V element, it will heat 40 gallons of oil to 140°F in about 2 to 4 hours. Or you can buy a second setup, install that in the barrel also, and cut the time in half.

Following are instructions on how to build this.

LEFT TO RIGHT: BOX EXTENSION, MUD RING, THERMOSTAT AND COUPLER, THERMOSTAT

MATERIALS LIST

Heating element (240V will heat much more quickly but may be too hot and burn out fast; I recommend a 110V, 1500W element). *Note*: Don't try running a 240V element on 110V. It'll work, but it will put out less than a 110V element on a true 110V circuit.

— Thermostat for the heating element. Don't get the kind that comes in a plastic mounting pad. Get one with mounting tabs that you can run a screw through.
— Steel electrical box extension. These are open on the back and allow it to surround the heating element and thermostat.
— Mud ring for a 4-gang opening. Allows you to adjust the thermostat but keeps you away from the exposed wiring.
— Wiring (get the correct gauge for your element).
— 1" black iron steel coupler that will thread onto the heater element.

Safety Tip: We've seen oil catch fire when using a 220V element when we had only about 1" of oil over it. Such an element gets hot enough to catch the oil on fire, but in our experiments a 110V, 1500W element does not.

Check with your hardware or electrical person for other items needed. You may need some other electrical box fittings in order to complete this.

ASSEMBLY

Take a sound 55-gallon barrel and drill a hole in it, about 4" to 6" off the bottom, 1¼" in size (verify against your element, as it should be just large enough to allow the threads on your heating element to pass through). Then place the rubber gasket on the heating element and pass the element through the hole.

Next, take the 1" coupler and place it inside the barrel, over the element. Tighten it down on the element until the gasket has sealed tightly to the barrel. *Note:* You might have to "flatten" the barrel slightly to make the gasket fit tightly. Some people weld a threaded bung on the barrel, which might be better but takes more work and skill.

Tip: If you use this barrel to "preheat" your oil before pumping it into the processor, be aware that you'll lose about 10–15°F of heat from pumping hot oil into a cold tank through cold pipes. So you might want to heat the oil up to about 145°F, and it will then cool 10 to 15 degrees once it starts circulating in the tank. Experiment with your tank to determine your heat losses.

Now you'll have to hook up the electrical box extension to the tank so that the box fits tightly against the element nut and still leaves room for the thermostat inside the box. You may have to align things somewhat diagonally, or whatever fits. This ring is meant only to help avoid accidental shorting of the exposed wires. The thermostat should be above the element, to read the heat correctly. See the photo.

Finally, wire the element to the thermostat. Then wire the whole thing to your household circuit. **I STRONGLY SUGGEST that you get an electrician to help you here, for safety.** Or at least get advice from an electrician, as we're not qualified to tell you how to wire this into your household wiring. I also recommend hooking up the

BARREL HEATER WIRING

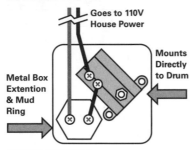

Goes to 110V House Power

Mounts Directly to Drum

Metal Box Extention & Mud Ring

WIRING EXAMPLE

element to a separate breaker if possible. Or, wire it into a spring-wound timer like an Intermatic model FF4h, as I believe these can handle a 1500W load. The timer is a great way to go, as you can then set it for 4 hours at night, and leave it be. It will easily heat to about 165°F, then shut off and allow the watery oil to settle out. The next morning it will have dropped to around 120°F, requiring minimal reheating to bring it up to temperature.

USE A BARREL BAND HEATER

This type of heater consists of bands that fit around the barrel and transfer heat into the oil through the tank wall. Such a heater is thermostatically controlled, but tends to be somewhat slow at heating cold cooking oil. To speed things up, you can stack several

heaters on the barrel. They generally cost somewhere around $150, so they're a lot more expensive than the previous option, but a good choice if you don't want to build a barrel heater as described above.

BARREL BAND HEATER

BUILD A HEAT EXCHANGE SYSTEM

You could build some type of heater that uses a heat exchange method. This could be something like a water heater that sends hot water through lines running into the processor through a series of coils and returns the water to the heater. This transfers the heat from the water to the oil without directly heating the oil.

You could build a heater that heats the oil via heating elements outside the processor. It would incorporate heating elements in an external enclosure through which you pump the oil. The oil passing over the heating elements heats the oil directly. This method also requires a thermostat. Even with a thermostat, there's a risk of overheating the oil, since water heater thermostats aren't meant to precisely control the temperature. They can have an allowance of 10° to 15°F, so be careful if you build this type of heater; otherwise, invest in a more expensive, but more precise, thermostat setup.

TRANSFERRING THE OIL TO THE PROCESSOR

Once the oil reaches the desired temperature, you're ready to transfer it to the processor. Most people do this with the processor mixing pump. They incorporate some ball valves that allow them to draw the oil from the heating barrel, temporarily bypassing the bottom opening of the processor. You could also just dump the oil in the top, if you have a poly type processor, and you can probably pump it in with a hand-operated barrel pump (I haven't tried it, as the electric pump is easier and costs about the same). Be sure to avoid the bottom 4'' to 6'' of oil in your heating/dewatering barrel, as that's where the sludge and watery oil has settled during the dewatering step.

Once the oil is at the desired level in your tank, run the pump for 10 minutes to ensure that the oil is thoroughly mixed so that when you do your titration, it's done on a good, "average" sample of oil.

SAMPLE SYSTEM LAYOUT & FLUID FLOW
Using a cone bottom processor

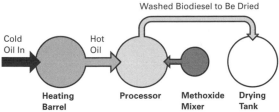

Washed Biodiesel to Be Dried

Cold Oil In · Hot Oil

Heating Barrel · **Processor** · **Methoxide Mixer** · **Drying Tank**

HOW THE FLUID FLOWS WHEN PROCESSING BIODIESEL

Tip: When filling the processing tank, always leave enough room for the 22 percent methoxide, *plus* a little additional room at the top of the tank. This space is important, so as to allow the misters to stay the proper distance away from the fuel. If they get too close, they can emulsify the fuel due to the more aggressive spray up close.

Pump Notes: Make sure you prime the pump correctly first, getting *all* the air out of the pump. If you can fill the output line above the pump, it will work even better, because the pump will "bleed" air into this oil, and then the oil can refill the pump until it fully primes. Also, *don't* mount your pump vertically, as seen on some processors. This makes it impossible to use the priming port, and very difficult to get it primed. I know, because I tried. About the only way to prime with this setup is to use your shop vacuum, and who wants to do that? Once we located the pump horizontally and lower to the ground, it worked much better. After you've filled the tank, it will stay primed, as a result of the flooding action of the oil in the tank being higher than the pump. But mount it slightly higher than the output at the bottom of the tank, so that you can drain the pump of any glycerine after it has settled out.

DOING A TITRATION ON THE OIL

First, circulate the oil from the bottom of the tank and back in the top for 10 minutes, to thoroughly mix the oil for a good, "average" test result. After the oil has mixed for 10 minutes, it's time to do a titration. You can get a sample of oil out through a dedicated drain you built into your system; or, if using an open-top system, you can just reach in and take a sample. Whichever way you do it, get about a cupful so that it retains its heat while testing.

Then perform the titration test as outlined in Chapter 4, or use the handy quick reference guide on page 165.

MIXING THE CATALYST AND METHANOL TOGETHER

After doing the titration, you should have used the biodiesel calculator from our website (*www.ezbiodiesel.com/bookbonus.htm*) to calculate the amount of methanol and catalyst to mix together. Or you could have manually calculated the methanol at 22 percent of the volume of oil being processed, and then used the KOH titration sheet in the back of the book to calculate the KOH. You can now mix the methanol and catalyst in your methoxide mixing tank. Once mixed, they're commonly referred to collectively as "methoxide."

> *CAUTION: THIS IS ONE OF THE MOST DANGEROUS PROCEDURES WE DO, SO WEAR ALL YOUR SAFETY GEAR!*

If you're using an Appleseed reactor, the common method is to mix the methoxide in one or two carboys by gently rocking them every 5 to 10 minutes over the course of about 30 minutes or more.

If you have a dedicated mixing tank, first add the methanol, then begin to add the lye or KOH and mix very thoroughly. **IMPORTANT: DON'T** add the catalyst all at once, as it can start "boiling" and splattering, possibly causing **SEVERE BURNS**. Add it slowly over at least 15 to 30 seconds; it will mix better that way, too. Don't mix the methoxide manually in an open-top container, as this mixture can burn you very quickly from even a minor splash. Again, I urge you to be extra careful during this procedure.

TRANSFERRING THE METHOXIDE TO THE PROCESSOR

Once mixing of the methoxide is complete and you have the oil at the proper temperature, it's time to add the methoxide. To do this, first start the pump on the processor and get the oil circulating. Then slowly open the valve, which lets the methoxide into the intake side of the pump. You want the methoxide to enter slowly, ensuring that it gets distributed all throughout the oil as it circulates (15 to 20 minutes is a normal duration). Once you add the methoxide, you should see the oil on the output side of the pump turn very turbid, looking a bit like foamy cola. This is normal. Your flow will probably even slow down quite a bit for a while, then it should speed back up a little. As more and more methoxide enters the oil flow, it begins to thin the oil down with the methanol, so your flow should begin picking up as more methoxide is added. It will also get darker and will lose the foamy look as this happens.

Tip: Once all the methoxide has been added, your pump might start sucking air, which could cause it to lose its prime. You want to be around when it's about done emptying, so that you can shut the valve off when it starts sucking air.

AGITATING AND MIXING THE METHOXIDE AND OIL

Agitation is one of the key elements of making biodiesel. This action helps to mix the methoxide thoroughly into the oil, ensuring a complete reaction throughout. The agitation must be strong enough

AGITATION ACTION INSIDE A CONE BOTTOM TANK WHEN MAKING BIODIESEL

to keep the methoxide thoroughly mixed into the oil, maximizing the methoxide/oil interaction.

The amount of time the batch must mix depends on the oil temperature. As discussed in the "Heating the Oil" section, the warmer the oil is, the less time you must "agitate" it to achieve a complete reaction. We determine the mixing time according to the oil's temperature when all the methoxide has been added. Use the times below, which are the times currently recommended by the University of Idaho Department of Biological and Agricultural Engineering.

RECOMMENDED MIXING TIMES

80°F = 4 to 8 hours
105°F = 2 to 4 hours
120°F = 2 to 3 hours
140°F = 1 to 2 hours

You should always process on the high side of the recommended time as a safety factor, to ensure that you don't cut it too close. This doesn't hurt, and can help guarantee a complete reaction.

Other variables can affect the overall time also: how fast your pump runs, whether the methoxide simply flows into the tank or is forced in under some pressure, and so on. If you don't mix long enough, to say it once more, you'll end up with an incomplete reaction.

Tip: If you reduce the pump output line as it enters the tank, this will speed up the flow and pressure. This can be done by using a reducing fitting on the line inside the tank. Then out of that comes a pipe of one size smaller. *Example:* Say the lines coming

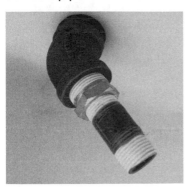

out of your pump are ¾" in size. Inside the tank you would reduce that down to ½" as it's pumped into the tank. It won't flow any more gallons per minute, but it *will* discharge at a higher pressure and *will* come out faster, giving the effect of a stronger pump. Angling the input, if done right, can also help get the oil swirling inside the tank.

EXAMPLE OF REDUCER INSIDE PROCESSOR

SETTLING

The next important point in the process involves settling the glycerine out of the oil, leaving behind the biodiesel. This is the step after you've run the pump and mixed the methoxide into the oil. After the pump shuts off, you simply let it settle. This is one step where you actually don't do anything. But it's is still an important step to understand. How long is up to you, but 10 to 12 hours is a bare minimum. For higher-quality fuel, 24 to 48 hours may allow more glycerine and debris to settle out. The majority of the glycerine will actually settle out in less than an hour, but by settling 10 to 12 hours you'll get a higher percentage to settle out before draining. Glycerine will actually continue to settle out for weeks, though the

GLYCERINE HAS SETTLED TO THE BOTTOM OF THE BIODIESEL

amount that settles out each day decreases substantially. Once we begin the water wash, this stops the chemical reaction and thereby halts the glycerine-forming and settling process. It's important to stop the settling, otherwise glycerine can continue to settle in your fuel tank and eventually you'll have a little puddle in there, causing you problems.

Tip: No matter what amount of time you let the mixture settle, you might want to drain most of the glycerine off every 3 to 4 hours, especially in cold weather. Why? The glycerine can start to thicken in the bottom and may become somewhat difficult to drain. If you use lye this can be more of a problem, but if you use KOH, it will be more likely to remain liquid.

DRAINING THE GLYCERINE

After you've allowed the mixture to settle for the desired time, the next step is to drain the byproduct of glycerine and dispose of it. Simply drain it into a bucket and discard it in your preferred way.

LAYERS FROM TOP TO BOTTOM—
BIODIESEL, WATER, GLYCERINE—
SHOW HOW EACH HAS ITS OWN
DENSITY

(See Chapter 8 for tips on disposal.) If your processor is high enough off the ground (the bottom fittings should be about 16" to 20" above the ground to work), you can even drain the glycerine directly into a 55-gallon drum.

When draining, stop as soon as you see an oily yellow film start coming out, or a liquid that's lighter and slightly more golden in color than the glycerine, as this indicates that you're draining biodiesel. (If it's creamy yellow, it could be an emulsion layer; see the "Emulsions" section in

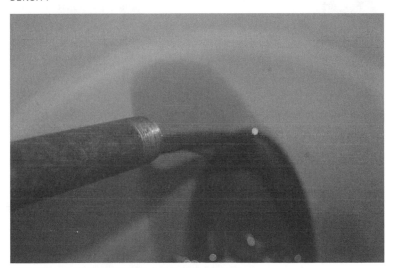

DRAINING GLYCERINE INTO A 5-GALLON BUCKET

Chapter 10 for more.) In the final draining, drain a little extra to get all the water out, but for now you can stop early.

At this point you should also drain the pump, since it should still have biodiesel in it, containing glycerine at the bottom. Just close off the tank valve and drain the pump. Then later, flush it with some washed biodiesel and drain again to make sure that no glycerine is left behind.

Tip: When draining, drain all but the last gallon or so, then stop. Wait 1 or 2 minutes for the biodiesel/glycerine layer to stabilize, then finish draining. You might want to hold on to the last 5 or 10 gallons until you're done washing, in case you have an emulsion. You can use the glycerine to help break an emulsion.

WATER WASHING

NOTICE HOW THE WATER SETTLES EASILY TO THE BOTTOM

Washing is an important step, as it helps to remove the impurities left behind by the transesterification process. These impurities can cause damage to your engine and must be removed. Unwashed fuel will *never* come close to meeting ASTM specifications. Washing removes contaminants such as soap, methanol, excess catalyst, free glycerine, and water-soluble impurities. In addition to the possible engine damage, these impurities can cause the biodiesel to retain free water, which leads to further problems.

As mentioned earlier, washing also helps halt the reaction so that no further glycerine drops out in your fuel tanks.

Homebrewers do their washing most often by using either bubble washing (developed at the University of Idaho) or mist washing. Most biodiesel makers looking to make premium-quality biodiesel do both. Although mist washing isn't absolutely necessary, when you mist wash first, you reduce the chance of an emulsion, because mist washing agitates the biodiesel less than bubble washing. Since this first wash removes a large part of the soaps and any contaminants, successive washes have less chance to form an emulsion. Therefore, start with a mist washing first, then finish with several bubble washes.

DRY WASHING

An alternative to water washing, dry washing solves several problems that you might run into when water washing, but it also creates a few of its own.

Dry washing most often involves using either Magnesol or Amberlite, both of which become a side stream in and of itself. Magnesol is magnesium silicate in a synthetic form; basically, it's a special talc that adsorbs moisture and contaminants and can reduce the amount of washing required. Magnesol is a trademarked product of the Dallas Group of America and is referred to as an "adsorbent filter aid" that ensures biodiesel quality by removing contaminants within methyl esters. (Methyl ester is the technical name of biodiesel made with methanol.) Amberlite is essentially plastics-ionized resins that remove impurities in your fuel.

To use Magnesol, you typically drain the glycerine, then add the required amount of Magnesol and stir for about 20 minutes. Then the Magnesol is filtered out and you're done. I've heard that it can be very difficult to remove all the Magnesol, but the manufacturer says it's not; I haven't yet verified that by testing. Also, it can be used in conjunction with water washing to reduce the costs. If you did a water wash to start with, you could likely use less Magnesol. Or, if you finished off with a water wash, you could probably reduce the filtering requirements.

To use Amberlite, the process is slightly different. Since this is a product consisting of resin beads, you have to flow the biodiesel through the Amberlite in a column. The beads absorb the impurities until they reach saturation or become clogged, at which point you replace the beads with new ones. More information can be found in the Resources section.

The chief problem with dry washing methods is that they will raise the price of your fuel by 1 to 10 cents per gallon, probably on the higher side for homebrewers. Yet it will take less time to wash, so the tradeoff is higher cost for more production. Then there's the disposal issue. You no longer have water to dispose of, but instead you've got spent Magnesol. So far the standard advice from the manufacturers of both products, when asked about disposal, is "just landfill them." There may turn out to be uses for the remnant product as animal feed, fertilizer, or composting. These ideas still seem to be under analysis. The final concern is whether we can remove *all* the Magnesol, or are instead leaving some very fine, abrasive particles in our fuel. We at EZBiodiesel are still analyzing this new method and will post our conclusions on our website.

WHAT'S NEEDED FOR BOTH WATER WASH METHODS (MIST WASHING AND BUBBLE WASHING)

Misting system—This basically just requires a misting head and the fittings to install it and be able to attach a water line to it. We've found the single-head misters to be of better quality, as they clog less and are much more durable. You can find a choice of these online. One thing to keep in mind: Avoid plain steel anywhere in the plumbing of the mister, as the metal will rust and the rust will

MISTING NOZZLE

clog the misting head. Stick with brass, plastic, or stainless.

Aquarium air pump—Look for one rated for about the same size tank as the amount of biodiesel you're making. If you get one slightly too big, you can turn down the pump speed, but you can't make a small one put out more—so err on the slightly larger size. Be sure to mount the pump higher than the liquid level, to avoid siphoning back into the pump and ruining it. Or install a check valve in the line (one usually comes with the air pump). An adjustable air valve is handy for controlling the air flow rate, also.

Aquarium air stone—Get a large one, as it will sink to the bottom more easily and put out a good volume of air over a larger area. Don't buy a stone with plastic around it, as the biodiesel will likely melt the plastic (it happened to me). The limewood

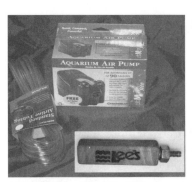

AIR BUBBLER, AIR LINE, AND LIMEWOOD BUBBLER

like a threaded steel nut. Homemade bubblers usually don't work
well, for they tend to produce too large a bubble. The holes need to
be extremely tiny, as small bubbles work better and agitate less.

Air line tubing—Buy a roll of tubing to hook all this up. Note
that most aquarium tubing will harden in the biodiesel after making
just 5 or 6 tanks of fuel, so expect to replace it often. Our processors
come with a special hose we buy in bulk, which holds up much
longer.

Timer—*Optional*. For a few dollars, you can add a timer to the
pump to turn it off several hours before you'll be checking on it.
This lets more contaminants and water settle out before you drain
the water. If you run the bubbler too long, this can emulsify the
biodiesel or turn the wash water into something resembling
whipped cream, making a timer a good idea.

MIST WASHING

To mist wash, start by adding a ratio of roughly 25 percent water to
your biodiesel, using your misting system. For example, if you made
20 gallons of biodiesel, add about 5 gallons of water (or more), using
the misting heads. Warm, softened water is best, though tap water
can be used. Be sure to add the water very gently or you could risk
emulsion. (See the "Emulsions" definition in Chapter 10.) (See
examples of an emulsion on our website, *www.ezbiodiesel.com/
bookbonus.htm*.)

Then, after misting in all the required water, allow the water to
settle out of the biodiesel for about 10 minutes, drain it into a 5-
gallon bucket, then dispose of the water. When draining, stop as
soon as you see yellow start coming out, which means you're
draining biodiesel. In the final draining, I like to drain a little extra
to get all the water out, but for now, stop early. The mist washing is
done. Note that a mister that sprays too fast or too hard can easily
emulsify the fuel. I once tried a three-head mister that was just too
aggressive, and it emulsified the batch. I've tried garden sprayers,
with the same results. So stick with a good mister that makes a *very
fine*, gentle spray.

Note: The biodiesel will sometimes go from a dark amber color to
an orange juice color. *Don't worry*, as it's just water that's
suspended in the fuel, mostly by the remaining soap and methanol.
It'll get a little darker again with each wash, and then even darker

when you dry it. See our website photo gallery for examples of this (*www.ezbiodiesel.com/bookbonus.htm*). This often panics people new to making biodiesel.

BUBBLE WASHING

BUBBLING THE BIODIESEL

To bubble wash, start by adding about 25 percent water to your biodiesel. You can mist it in again, add it with a garden hose turned way down to avoid agitation, siphon it in with a bucket and hose, or use an aquarium pump to pump it in. Because the water is heavier than the biodiesel, it will immediately sink to the bottom. Misting it in the second time is safest, but you can use a hose to speed things up. Whenever you use any kind of hose, put it close to the biodiesel layer (or even in it) and add the water slowly. Going too fast or agitating it too much risks emulsifying the biodiesel. A garden hose will work, if you're careful; try putting a garden bubbler on the end, which breaks up the flow and makes it less aggressive.

Next, lower the aquarium bubbler to the bottom of the tank into the water layer. Make sure it actually sinks, as some smaller ones need to be weighted down.

Tip: Between each bubble wash, drain the wash water and dispose of it. Most people dump it on the ground, or down the municipal sewer drain (not down a storm drain, as most of them go straight to a river or bay).

First bubble wash—Leave the water in the bottom and immediately begin the first bubble wash, to run for about 1 to 5 hours. Just set your timer (if you have one) and start the air pump for the desired amount of time.

The higher your oil titrated at, the less time you should bubble it. *Example:* Oil that titrates at less than 1 can usually be bubbled for 5 hours the first time. If it titrated from 1 to 3, start with 3 hours; from 3 up start with 1 hour. Make sure it doesn't bubble too vigorously this first time, otherwise you could end up with an emulsion, which is bad. Big bubbles, or too many too fast, *will often emulsify biodiesel*. If you need to, you can either vary the air output on the pump, or pinch the hose down a little to reduce the bubbles to a gentle flow. Let this process complete, then settle for 30 minutes, before draining the wash water. The settling time is optional, but does allow more contaminants to settle out.

Second bubble wash—Do another bubble wash just like the first one, only a little longer this time. Usually *double* the first time works out well. If you go too long, you can still risk an emulsion, so watch it carefully every now and then if you go for longer times. (This is due to the soap that's accumulating in the wash water as it bubble washes.)

Repeat bubble washes—You can do one to three more bubble washes; just keep doubling the time you used last time, going as long as 12 to 24 hours total (more won't hurt for the final washes). Keep washing until the drain water coming out is *almost* perfectly clear and measures close to the same pH as tap water. I drain some water into a small, clear container to examine it easier. (*Note:* The water may have tiny bubbles, making it look slightly cloudy. Let it sit and they should disappear if it's actually clear, though it may never come out totally clear.) If you're unsure whether it's clean, do one more wash and compare to the previous one. If it's cleaner this time, you needed this wash. If not, the previous wash was as good as it gets.

DRY WASHING (OPTIONAL)

See the section on page 153.

DRYING THE WASHED FUEL

After washing your biodiesel, it will usually have a slightly hazy or cloudy appearance to it and will typically be more orange colored than dry biodiesel. This is because your just-washed biodiesel contains microdroplets of water still in suspension. Because of its ability to absorb water, biodiesel can hold water in suspension at up to 1,500 ppm (parts per million), which works out to 0.15 percent (well above the ASTM level of 0.05 percent). But, even at that level your biodiesel should look clear. After washing, it looks very cloudy because the percentage of water it's holding is very high, much higher than 1,500 ppm. Therefore, we need to remove as much water as possible before we use it.

BIODIESEL IN THE DRYING BARREL
BEFORE DRYING

BIODIESEL IN THE DRYING BARREL
AFTER DRYING

To dry the biodiesel after washing it, you can simply leave it in an open-top barrel for several days to a week or more. It will eventually dry this way unless you're in a very humid or cold climate.

Or, to dry it much faster, you can use a dedicated drying setup. To do this, use an open-top 55-gallon drum and a fan to air dry it. If you can find a way to pump the fuel in a circulation mode into and out of the tank, and can make the fuel "fan" out, it will dry faster. See the "fan drying" photo on this page. Anything that will spread the fuel out to increase the surface area will help. It works this way: Use a pump to recirculate the biodiesel in and out of the open-top barrel (often the processor pump doubles as the drying pump), and as it sprays back into the tank you spray it out in a fan shape. If you have an actual fan blowing toward the drying area, the drying action will be speeded up, because the moving air will carry more moisture away faster. The fuel will usually dry in 2 to 4 hours this way.

If you use the processor pump, you can also use its timer to control the drying time.

In high-humidity areas or on colder days, you might want to use a 300W aquarium heater, which will heat the biodiesel to 90°F. If you do this, *be careful,* as the heater can melt through a plastic

AIR DRYING BIODIESEL WITH FAN
DRYER

drum. Just suspend it in the middle and you should be fine.

You'll know when the fuel is dry, as it will go from very hazy to very clear—not colorless, but clear. You should be able to hold it up in a clear container such as a water bottle, next to some printed text, and read the text through the biodiesel. (View large color examples of this on our website.) If you've been heating the fuel, the heat could cause the fuel to clear up, because warmer fuel will look clearer than cold fuel if there's any water in it. This is because as the fuel heats up, it will hold more water in suspension, making the

READING TEXT THROUGH WASHED AND DRIED BIODIESEL

fuel look clear. So be sure it's actually dry by running the pump another hour or so. Then if it cools down and stays clear (above 40°F), it's in fact dry. Don't get carried away, though, or you could overdo it and possibly cause oxidative stability problems. This is more a problem if you'll be storing the fuel a long time, and not a real problem for short-term storage.

Remember, the color of your finished fuel can vary. This isn't truly important, as biodiesel can range from dark amber to almost clear, depending on the type of oil.

Tip: When drying, don't put the fan too close or you'll likely blow a "biodiesel mist" all over. Practice makes perfect. Also, take care to run the pump as slowly as possible while maintaining the fan spray, because excess agitation of the wet biodiesel can sometimes cause a foaminess on the surface; this can coagulate a little on the tank sidewalls, leaving behind a gummy residue.

Some people have been experimenting with bubbling air through the fuel with the aquarium air bubbler, and they end up with sparkling-clear fuel. But the jury is still out on whether the fuel is actually dry or something else is going on.

After the biodiesel is dry, you should transfer it to sealed storage containers as soon as possible. Reason: Biodiesel is hygroscopic and will start to reabsorb moisture if left in an open container.

FINAL SETTLING

To achieve the best fuel, you can let the finished product settle in a closed barrel for several days to several weeks. What this does is let any final impurities settle out. This method works well, and by getting ahead of your fuel needs you'll be able to do this and also end up with slightly higher-quality fuel. *Note:* It's best to store it in a sealed, full barrel to avoid unwanted moisture absorption, as biodiesel *will* absorb moisture from the air. Store it out of direct sunlight, too. Usually you won't get much to settle out, but it's a good way to settle out contaminants caused by drying or just something that got by the washing process. It's basically a safety measure and not strictly necessary if the fuel is very high quality.

FINAL FILTERING

FILTERING IS DONE AT YOUR OWN FILLING STATION

The final filtering is done when you pump the fuel out for use. Depending on your pump setup, you can put a filter on the output line of your pump and simply filter as you dispense it. Filtering it as you use it produces the cleanest fuel. Most people use a water block Goldenrod or Wix fuel filter, but almost any fuel filter setup should work. Note that a water block fuel filter is *not* a substitute for drying. For one reason, it won't hold enough and will clog too often. For another reason, it's rated "nominally," meaning that a fairly large percentage of the water will get past it. Since the process of washing the fuel leaves a large amount of water in the fuel, trying to filter it out would be ineffective due to the nominal rating as well as fuel filters' capacity.

Filtering to 10 microns is considered good enough for diesel engines, though you can go finer if you wish. I suggest keeping a spare filter on hand, to avoid having to run to the parts store when it finally clogs up.

80/20 PROCESSING METHOD

I want to mention another method, even though you may not use it. This method, called the "80/20 processing method," is supported by the University of Idaho experts as a way to improve the reaction rates. To do an 80/20 process involves doing the reaction in two steps: First, you prepare everything like you normally do, including the mixing of the methoxide. But when you start adding the methoxide to the oil, you only add 80 percent of the methoxide and run the processor about 1 to 2 hours. After the pump shuts off, you wait for the majority of the glycerine to drop out (usually about 30 minutes), then you drain the glycerine in the usual manner. Next you add the remaining 20 percent of the methoxide and process the oil again. Overall, it takes a little more work, but you should see a higher conversion ratio, and therefore less "bound" glycerine in your fuel.

The reason this works is fairly simple. By processing with 80 percent of the methoxide first, and then draining the glycerine, you're able to remove a large part of the total glycerine. Then when you add the remaining 20 percent of the methoxide, the mixture doesn't have all that glycerine in there fighting the reaction. Normally, the glycerine in the batch is basically interfering with the reaction. By removing about 80 percent of it in the first process, you allow the remaining methoxide to more completely work on breaking down the remainder of the triglycerides as there's very little glycerine to interfere.

Here's the 80/20 process, step by step:

1 Heat your oil as usual.
2 Titrate your oil as usual.
3 Measure the required catalyst and methanol as usual, and mix well.
4 Add only 80 percent of your methoxide into your oil.
5 Run the processor for 1 to 2 hours.
6 Just before turning off the pump, take a small sample. Observe how fast the glycerol is separating from your partially reacted biodiesel. Once the glycerol has separated, wait about 5 more minutes and drain the glycerine from your reactor. Normally, the total time needed for glycerol separation is only 15 to 30 minutes.
7 Now add the remaining 20 percent of the methoxide. This should take 10 to 15 minutes.

8   Run the processor for another 3 hours.

9   Settle overnight.

10 The next day, drain the remaining glycerine and continue washing and drying as usual.

NOTES ON HEATING THE BIODIESEL WORKSPACE

You should try to do all this in a well-heated shop. I always heat our shop to about 80°F and hold it there during the reaction and washing stages. If you do the same, make sure the heater for your shop isn't a possible ignition source in the event that some methanol vapors escape. If it is, heat the shop extra well before starting, then turn off the heater for the rest of the process.

You may want to build a small room in your shop to house the processor. That way, in the winter you only have to heat this small room, which a small electric baseboard heater will do efficiently. Often, all you have to do is to frame two walls in a corner and, using existing outside walls and the existing ceiling, presto: You have a room. Of course you'll need a door, but you can frame your own shed-type door or pick up a cheap door at a salvage yard. If you insulate it well, it won't take much to heat it in the winter, and it will hold the heat better. Consider framing it from 2x6 studs, letting you fit more insulation in the wall cavities. Also, caulk all possible air leaks, such as the bottom plate where it meets the floor, any openings, and the like.

Heat lamps can add a fair amount of heat to a cold room. They work best if within a few feet of the tanks, but you have to be careful. A bulb that breaks will spark, which could be dangerous. Therefore, mount the light securely, and use a shielded light fixture. Don't put the light too close to the tank or it can melt (if MDPE), but only when closer than about 10 inches.

You might even consider having a loop from your home heater run into your biodiesel room. Heating a room this size should consume little power.

Alternatively, you can build your own waste oil heater and incorporate that into heating your shop. Then you'll have all the heat you want for free, as you can use waste motor oil, waste veggie oil, and other types, to heat even a fairly large shop. See the Resources section for more information on a waste oil heater you can build at home, as well as commercial grade waste oil heaters.

You likely can come up with many more ideas for having a warm biodiesel room during the winter. You could even insulate a small enclosed trailer and make biodiesel in that.

TIMELINE FOR THE ENTIRE PROCESS

Here is a rough guide of the time you could spend making biodiesel, from start to finish. I won't include getting the oil, since that varies too much and can be done with other errands, reducing the overall time involved. The times listed below are only *estimates* of your actual hands-on time for a given step, not including any waiting time.

TIME LINE EXAMPLE FOR A 40-GALLON BATCH

Assumes you are near your processor the whole day. If not, time line will be off, but the hands-on time will be accurate.

Time:	OPERATION DESCRIPTION - DAY 1	Actual Hands-on Time
8 a.m.	Turn on heaters to reheat the oil (still warm from dewatering the day before)	3 minutes 3 minutes
8.30	Transfer the oil to the mixing tank and circulate for 10 minutes. *Note:* While the oil is circulating, you can add more oil to the heating barrel and begin dewatering this batch if you want.	5 minutes
8:45	Perform 2 or 3 titrations.	3 minutes
8:50	Calculate the amount of lye and methanol, using the biodiesel calculator.	3 minutes
8:55	Add the methanol and lye to the mixing tank, then let it mix for 15 to 20 minutes (using KOH).	5 minutes
9:15	Now start the processor pump and begin adding the methoxide over about 15 minutes. You can then set the timer for the proper time according to our guide, and let it run by itself.	15 minutes
	TOTAL HANDS-ON TIME:	34 minutes

Time:	OPERATION DESCRIPTION - DAY 2	Actual Hands-on Time
8 a.m.	Drain the glycerine from the processor.	5 minutes
8:10	Hook up the mister, set the mist water timer, and begin misting.	2 minutes
10:00	Drain the mist water.	3 minutes
10:05	Add more water (approximately 20 to 25% of the biodiesel volume), using our quick-fill setup, and start the bubble washing.	4 minutes
12:30 p.m.	Drain the first bubble wash water .	3 minutes
12:35	Add more water as done previously, and start another bubble wash for about 5 or 6 hours.	4 minutes
6:30	Drain the second bubble wash water.	3 minutes
6:35	Add more water and start the final bubble wash, to run overnight.	4 minutes
	TOTAL HANDS-ON TIME:	28 minutes

Time:	OPERATION DESCRIPTION - DAY 3	Actual Hands-on Time
8 a.m.	Drain the final bubble wash water from the day before.	3 minutes
8:05	Transfer the fuel to the drying tank.	4 minutes
8:15	Once the biodiesel is in the drying tank, set the correct valves and begin circulating to dry the biodiesel for 2 to 4 hours, depending on temperatures and humidity. At this point, you just let it run for several hours. Check it after several hours and if it's clear, it's dry. You can now let it settle either in this tank or a separate settling tank (the latter is only needed for higher production rates).	1 minutes
	Last step is to transfer it to your final dispensing tank, using the processor's pump or your own separate pump, and then you're done.	5 minutes
	TOTAL HANDS-ON TIME:	13 minutes

TOTAL APPROXIMATE HANDS-ON TIME FOR ALL 3 DAYS:	75 minutes

Titration Quick Reference Guide

This is a quick reference guide for the shop. For detailed instructions, see the book. Be sure to use separate syringes or eyedroppers for each fluid, to avoid cross-contamination. *Note:* Items in bold are the four main steps, and amounts to remember.

1. Set out 3 mixing cups or jars. Label 2 of them "Reference" and "Titration." The third is to collect an oil sample.
2. Add *roughly* 6 to 10 tablespoons of reference solution into the "Reference" cup. The reference solution is EXACTLY 1 gram of catalyst in 1 liter of distilled water.
3. Using the wash bottle (squirt bottle), fill the 25 ml cylinder with exactly **20 ml of isopropyl alcohol**, then add this to the titration testing cup. (Fill wash bottle beforehand with the isopropyl alcohol and label it.)
4. Add 5 to 7 drops (or a quick squirt) of titration indicator to "Titration" cup and swirl until mixed well.
5. Do a blank titration by adding drops of the reference solution until alcohol changes color, then STOP. May take from 1 to 20 drops (if more, try new alcohol).
6. Using the sampling valve just above the pump, fill the third cup with warm oil.
7. Add exactly **2 ml of warm oil** into the "Titration" cup and mix well. Swirl the mixture around until the oil dissolves as much as possible (heating it up briefly may help).
8. Draw up exactly **5 ml of reference solution** into an eyedropper or syringe.
9. Begin adding drops of reference solution to the "Titration" cup and continue to swirl.
10. When the color changes to purple or pinkish and holds for 15 to 30 seconds, STOP. If you run out of the "Reference" solution first, just draw up 5 ml more and continue.
11. Note the TOTAL ml it took to reach this point and **divide it by 2**. Write this number down in the spaces below, using a china marker or grease pen (clean with alcohol).
12. Empty the "Titration" cup, wipe it dry with a paper towel, and repeat test 1 or 2 more times. Then write the numbers in the appropriate space below.

After 3 tests, use the 2 that came out closest to the same, and disregard the third. The average is your acid value (or titration) number for this oil. If the results are less than 3, the oil is very usable. If it's over that, see the book for more info.

1st test result   _____

2nd test result   _____

3rd test result   _____

Final titration number _____

Processing Instructions Overview

This is a simplified version of the book instructions. Use this as a reference only. If you need detailed instructions, please see the instructions in the book.

1. **Filter** – your oil into your heating barrel and dewater your oil overnight.
2. **Reheat the oil** – to about 145°F, then turn off the element.
3. **Transfer the oil** to your processor (leave the bottom 5" in the barrel).
4. **Circulate** – the entire mixture for 10 minutes with the lid on to retain heat.
5. **Titrate** – Perform 2 or 3 titration tests.
6. **Calculate the KOH** – Determine the KOH and methanol (22%) you need using the KOH chart or the biodiesel calculator (download from www.myezbiodiesel.com).
7. **Mix the KOH and methanol** – until COMPLETELY dissolved (10 min for KOH, much longer for lye).
8. **Add the methoxide** – Start the pump and slowly introduce the methoxide (by cracking valve #5). Should take about 15 minutes to get it all in. Don't go too fast.
9. **Circulate the mixture** – After methoxide is in the oil, set the timer for the proper amount of time, depending on how hot your oil is. The guideline is:
   - 80°F = 4 to 8 hours
   - 105°F = 2 to 4 hours
   - 120°F = 2 to 3 hours
   - 140°F = 1 to 2 hours
10. **Settle** – Let the whole batch settle for 8 to 48 hours. Longer is a little better.
11. **Drain** – the glycerin.
12. Mist wash – Begin a gentle mist washing as described in the book (roughly 2 hrs).
13. **Bubble wash** – Do from 2 to 5 bubble washes until water comes out clear.
14. **Dry the biodiesel** – with a full but flow, using the drying attachment.
15. **Settle the biodiesel** – for 1 to 3 days for optimally clean fuel.
16. **Transfer to storage** – Transfer all but the bottom 2" to 3" to a dispensing tank.
17. **Filter** – Filter the final product to 5 to 10 microns before adding to your vehicle, or do it "while" adding the fuel to your vehicle.

CHAPTER 8

DISPOSING OF GLYCERINE AND WASTEWATER

Whenever people make something, they often have things left over that they have to deal with or get rid of. The same is true of making biodiesel. You can't just make it, pump some into your tank, and drive off into the sunset. No, you'll need to deal with the aftermath—which includes disposing properly of the glycerine and the wastewater, and perhaps recovering some methanol as well. And you'd be well-advised to make some extra bucks, or save some, putting these "waste" products to good use. This chapter tells you how.

GLYCERINE DISPOSAL

Disposing of the glycerine can be one of the more difficult aspects of making biodiesel for homebrewers, and even for commercial producers. As you know by now, making biodiesel creates a byproduct of glycerine, also known as glycerol and as glycerin. Glycerine coming out of your processor is usually only 50 percent glycerol, 40 percent methanol, and 10 percent soap and catalyst.

Glycerine created using lye and methanol will harden over time (sometimes quite quickly), whereas glycerine created using KOH will stay liquid longer. This can be a definite advantage. But note that the degree of hardness the glycerine reaches has no correlation whatever to the quality of biodiesel you've made.

Before you try to use the glycerine for anything, it's best to always remove the methanol, for reasons of safety. You have several possible methods. There is misinformation on the Internet that suggests you can simply leave the glycerine in a bucket with no lid on it for a week and the methanol will evaporate. That's not true, because glycerine ends up with a hard film on the top that would prevent the methanol from escaping. I think that with liquid glycerine from KOH you *could* stir it every day for a week in a bucket outdoors and you could possibly accomplish the evaporation, but I haven't tried it.

Alternatively, you can first run the glycerine through a methanol recovery system. I'll discuss methanol recovery a little later.

Be aware that the byproduct of glycerine is laden with methanol. One way to dispose of it involves pouring it into 5-gallon buckets or cubees, leaving no air gaps at the top, and disposing of it properly at a landfill. If you store it over a long period, then you should make sure you either store it open to the air and stir it periodically so that most of the methanol can evaporate, or store it in closed containers with no air gap so the methanol can't evaporate. A man grinding on a tank partially filled with methanol-laden byproduct was killed by an explosion from the methanol, in the only known death related to biodiesel.

USES

Glycerine has a *great many* uses, probably hundreds of them—from making soap to animal food additives to grease removers and hand cleaners. Most of these products, however, require a *much purer form of glycerine than you'll end up with* in your biodiesel processing. Trying to purify it to those levels is somewhat expensive and difficult. So, instead of your making soap and other products, I have a great idea for you.

Make money with it. That's right, you can get about $1 per gallon for your glycerine by selling it as a humectant, or dust abatement treatment. Glycerine is hygroscopic, meaning that it draws moisture from the air. When sprayed on dusty roads, riding arenas, construction sites, and the like, it will continually draw a small amount of moisture into the soil or sand, helping to keep the dust down by minimizing water evaporation. It also works by coalescence, the process by which separate masses of miscible (able to mix together) substances seem to "pull" each other together whenever they make the slightest contact. This basically helps "lock" the particles together, yet without clumping or making a mess.

In the old days, road crews used to spray motor oil onto dirt roads to keep the dust down. Of course, we've learned that this isn't a wise (or inexpensive) thing to do, so the common method today is to use magnesium chloride. Glycerine, however, is very environmentally safe (when the methanol is removed first) and is reusing the byproduct of biodiesel, and therefore it's a win–win situation to use it on dust applications.

In arenas, dust can be a major nuisance as well as a health hazard. Arenas such as rodeo arenas often generate a lot of dust due to being outdoors. In addition, the continual pounding of the animals' hooves breaks down the sand or other footing material into fine particles that are easily airborne. Breathing all that dust is considered harmful to horses and people alike. So the common method is to water the arena before each use. This expends a lot of water and time, and in fact the arena will dry out within a few hours anyway, requiring yet more water and more time. One method that some arenas use to control dust is to apply magnesium chloride. This can dry a horse's frog and hooves out, which is hard on them. Also, in an outdoor arena, the first time it rains, the product washes away. Glycerine is much better for horses and won't wash away nearly as easily. We're doing some long-term tests, but information on using glycerine leads us to believe that an arena may only need to be treated once or twice per summer depending on the climate conditions.

With this idea, you could sell the glycerine straight, and let others spray it themselves, or you could sell it straight to someone who has a water truck. Spraying diluted glycerine instead of straight water, a water truck should be able to keep construction sites and new roads damp much longer, both saving them money and reducing the dust better than water alone. I believe water trucks can spray a more-diluted mixture of about 10 percent glycerine and 90 percent water. After spraying a few times, the level will build up to where crews should be able to cut their spraying down by at least half or more.

We've been experimenting with this as I write, but it seems to work well. And what a wonderful use it could be! Making up to $1 a gallon essentially reduces your methanol cost by $1 a gallon, since 1 gallon of methanol used nets about 1 gallon of glycerine byproduct. If you set up a sprayer and charge for the service of spraying people's roads and private or public arenas, you could earn a fair amount of money for your time, since you should only have to treat it once or twice a year.

SPRAYING GLYCERINE TO REDUCE DUST

Here are some tricks to make this work, and some tips as well:

The sprayer—Depending on your situation, this could be a 12V pump, or 110V if you have a vehicle with a power converter. You could spray it through one spray nozzle that will "fan" the spray out nice and wide, plus have a sufficient volume. (See photo for glycerine spraying setup.)

Tanks—You could put an IBC tote or large water tank in the back of a pickup truck and spray from that. Or just take a few spare closed-head drums and use them to hold your product.

Mixing—While you can get glycerine and water to mix, they don't really like to stay mixed. Instead, use the pump itself to circulate the mixture until all is mixed well, then start spraying. Just remix each time it's allowed to settle for 15 minutes or so.

Dilute it—You don't want to spray it straight, but instead mix it with about 60 percent water (for roads and arenas; for water trucks, try 90 percent water and let it build up).

Spray deeply enough—By spraying enough to wet the top ½'' to 1½'' or so, the surface should be wet enough.

Arenas—With arenas, you want a slightly deeper soak of about 1½''. After spraying, you want to lightly turn the soil or sand over to mix the dry soil underneath with the top saturated layer. Just turn over the top 3'' or so, and this will distribute the glycerine better, leaving 3 inches of lightly treated soil. I assume that anyone who owns an arena also owns some sort of tractor and tiller, disc, or harrow.

need to soak only the top ½''. On a driveway with gravel, I'd dilute
with at least 60 percent water, or more, to get a slightly thinned-out
glycerine so that it doesn't get oily. We sprayed our long gravel
driveway and found that after the majority of the water evaporated,
the glycerine was left on the top of the gravel. This was very thin
glycerine but it caused a *small* transfer of glycerine to our shoes,
which could track onto carpets. It was a minor matter, but we found
that a solution was to spray some leftover bubble wash water on
top to wash off the gravel. Or spray a little city water with a tiny bit
of soap in it (such as 1 teaspoon per 50 gallons). *Then*, it would be
best to drag the driveway to turn all the gravel over. We turned ours
over with our homemade drag (hog panel with railroad ties and
tires on it) behind our biodiesel-powered tractor. Now you have a
well-treated driveway that will have minimal dust problems for
quite some time.

OTHER USES

I can't forget to mention that you can make soap with glycerine. If
you made soap from all your glycerine left over after making
biodiesel, you'd have everyone you know well stocked for years. If
you're interested in this method, search the Internet for some soap
recipes from biodiesel glycerine. They're easy and fun to use.

At your local landfill you can often find a composting facility in
your area that's either commercial or free. They'll often accept the
glycerine, as the methanol in it actually feeds the compost bacteria.
Better yet, *compost it yourself*. Just don't add too much, or you'll
drown the compost.

Some wastewater treatment facilities will accept the glycerine
for use in their methane digesters. They use it to generate electricity,
turning an otherwise "waste" product into electricity.

Some people have tried burning glycerine in a home fireplace or
woodstove, by adding other material such as wood chips to it and
forming logs by using milk cartons or similar containers—though
with limited success. A new company is said to have been successful
with this idea, by using pressure to form the logs.

Other people are experimenting with vermiculture, whereby a
large worm bed is grown and the worms feed on the glycerine-rich
soil. Little is yet known about the success of this idea.

To use glycerine for a hand cleaner or degreaser, you could boil it for quite a while to remove the methanol. Once you've done that, it makes an excellent degreaser. Just don't use it as a cleaner until you remove the methanol, for safety reasons.

Large-scale producers like Archer Daniels Midland are planning on producing a propylene glycol and ethylene glycol substitute from the glycerine. Other businesses are looking at using it in animal feed, or as a fuel, or in various other ways. Most ideas are still in the testing stage, though the possibilities are endless.

See our website for more ideas as they become available.

Note: **DON'T** pour glycerine down your storm drain or into your sewer system, as most systems can't handle that much glycerine at a time. This could cause you problems—and big plumbing bills.

WASTEWATER DISPOSAL

When you're making biodiesel, the process of washing should remove the methanol either into the air or into your wash water. It's usually OK to dispose of wash water, diluted with fresh water, down the municipal sewer (toilet, tub, or floor drain). However, it is **NOT OK** to pour it down the rainwater runoff drains. It is **NOT OK** for larger producers, making more than 300 gallons a week, to pour their untreated wash water down any drain. If you're producing larger amounts of wash water, consult with your city's sewage treatment facility to determine what level of pretreatment they require. You may have to provide a few water samples to determine this. The first wash will be much more contaminated than the last, so this will matter.

One of the biggest concerns about proper disposal of wastewater is its high BOD content. Biochemical oxygen demand (BOD5) is a measure of the dissolved oxygen consumed during the biochemical oxidation of organic matter present in a substance, done over five days. In smaller amounts, BOD content poses no problem for wastewater treatment plants. But for larger amounts, you should talk to them about how they can treat your quantities, as their treatment systems depend on a specific level of oxygen. An aerobic (meaning "with air") treatment system is usually recommended. This type of treatment system puts out water that's as clean as the municipal waste treatment itself puts out, so it's very effective.

A new idea being tried is a permaculture method, whereby beneficial plants are introduced into the wastewater treatment area. These plants attract the "good" bacteria, which feed on the "bad" bacteria in the water. Through a series of drain ponds the water is eventually clean enough to return to the streams or ocean. You can search the Internet for more on this evolving idea.

Another inviting idea is to run wastewater through a still that removes the excess methanol and kills the bacteria. Then it could possibly be final-filtered through a sand-and-gravel bed in a leach-field type of system.

I have read much conflicting information about wastewater going into septic systems. Someone who installs commercial type septic systems and is very familiar with BODs told me it shouldn't be a problem in smaller amounts, since septic systems start out as anaerobic systems (meaning "without air"). The smaller amounts of methanol that might be in the wash water shouldn't hurt anything either. Yet without further testing we can't say for sure as septic systems are actually quite complex. So your best bet is probably to avoid putting much in a septic system

Another creative and money-saving idea is to add the wash water to the glycerine if you'll be spraying it. That way, instead of adding treated water, you can simply add the wash water and kill two birds with one stone. One, you're reducing your use of treated water overall. Two, you're avoiding dumping the water down the drain. Once sprayed and spread out over a large area, the BOD shouldn't be a problem anymore, but to date we don't have proof of this.

If you do this, keep in mind you'll likely have more water than you need, as you usually go through as much water (in volume) as the biodiesel you produce, or more. But you only produce about 10 to 20 percent as much glycerine, depending on whether you measure it before or after removing the methanol.

METHANOL RECOVERY

Now that you've dealt with matters like disposing of the glycerine and wastewater, you have some time on your hands. Recovering the methanol is a grand idea to use some of that time—for several reasons. Of course, the less methanol we let into the atmosphere, the better off we all are, and the better off the earth itself is. Another benefit is that if we recover the methanol from the biodiesel before washing it, the washing process will be easier. Since methanol is the most expensive of the chemicals we use to make biodiesel, recovering some of it can cut our total cost of making the biodiesel.

Alas, recovering the methanol is not overly simple or inexpensive to build. The process is basically distillation. It's quite similar to building an old-fashioned moonshine still to make liquor. You heat the mixture up high enough to cause the methanol to vaporize, but not the liquid it's in. Then you condense it into another, separate tank. There are several questions to ask yourself, however, when attempting to recover methanol:

— Are you getting a complete condensation? If not, where are the remaining vapors going? (Let's hope it's not back into your work area.)

— How pure is the methanol you're recovering? You may be getting water in your methanol, because methanol easily absorbs water.

— Is your recovery method completely safe? Methanol, like most fuels, doesn't burn until it's vaporized. To recover it, you have to vaporize it, creating potentially explosive fumes.

— Can you use one recovery system to recover the methanol from the glycerine, biodiesel, and wash water, or will you need separate units for each?

— Or, will you only recover from the glycerine?

— If recovering only from the biodiesel, will you have to pump it out of your wash tank into a recovery unit, and then back into the processor? If so, how will you accomplish this?

Methanol recovery is actually quite complicated, though on the surface it seems easy enough. Due to the many dangers of methanol recovery, in this book we won't go into any details about designs or methods. If you're interested in learning more about this subject, you can find a great deal of discussion on the Internet. Despite all the excited talk about it, we've found it difficult to locate an actual, quality design online that isn't inadequate at best—or dangerous at worst. So buyer beware. See the Resources section in the back of the book for some websites that can help you.

TESTING BIODIESEL FOR QUALITY

Now that you've finished the biodiesel-making process, you might want to perform some basic tests to find out the quality of your fuel. Unfortunately, most home tests are far from conclusive. Some may even be faulty, and give you the wrong message about your work. Therefore, I'll list a few tests that have been suggested on the Internet that you can do at home, to give you a *rough* idea of the quality. Use them as a possible indicator only, and don't be overly alarmed if you fail one, or find it difficult to ascertain the results.

LABORATORY TESTS

For the ultimate test, you should send a sample out to a fuel-testing laboratory and have it tested according to ASTM standards. The current standard in the U.S. is ASTM D6751. The full ASTM test actually consists of many individual ASTM tests. You have to get all the individual tests done to complete the ASTM D6751 test. A few examples of the individual tests are: Free and total glycerine – Cetane – Flash point – Cloud point – Acid number, plus a dozen or so other tests. A test will cost from $80 for a simple "Free and Total glycerine" test up to $1,200 for the full ASTM D6751 test (depending on whether you order one test, numerous tests, or the full test). These tests will tell you exactly what quality fuel you're making. See the Resources section for testing companies.

HOME TESTS

It's not necessary that you perform the following home tests, but feel free to do them if you're trying to get a feel for the quality of the fuel you're making, beyond just using it to zoom on down the road. If you live in a cold area, though, I would advise that you do the cold weather testing. Note that there are *no* accurate, definitive home tests you can do; you simply can't have the needed equipment, facilities, and expertise. Some tests might give you a rough idea of the fuel quality, but no test is nearly as accurate as an ASTM-standards test.

REPROCESS TEST

This is a crude test for both monoglycerides and diglycerides. See the Glossary for definitions of the two terms, and read Chapter 10 for ways to avoid having them in your fuel. You can do a reprocess test by using 1 liter of biodiesel, 75 ml of methanol, and 1 g or so of lye. Mix the lye and methanol as usual, then add to the biodiesel, and shake for about 20 seconds. Shake it 2 or 3 more times, over the course of about 5 to 10 minutes, then let it settle out.

After a few hours, see how much settled out. *You will get some glycerine*, no matter what, because of the methanol you added. If the glycerine looks watered down, that's probably a good sign. If you only get back about what you put in (and if it's very thin), you probably have fuel that has been reacted fairly completely. If you get back more, your fuel has not reacted completely. I repeat that this is a very crude test, so don't interpret the results as definitive.

COLD-WEATHER TESTING

Biodiesel has an inherently higher cloud point (see Glossary) than does petrodiesel. Biodiesel will begin to develop cloudiness from around the low 20s Fahrenheit to the mid-40s, compared to diesel, which averages around 15°F (nonwinterized). You might want to test your biodiesel so that you know at what temperatures it will flow.

for more information on additives, blending, and so forth.) Be aware
that each restaurant's oil will likely have a different cloud point due
to the amount of tallows, the type of oil, and the like. So test each
one, and use only the best for winter oil.

Basically, to test your biodiesel for cold-weather performance,
you need to make up some control samples, then place them in a
controlled environment such as a refrigerator or freezer, with an
accurate thermometer, and see what happens. It's best to use an old
refrigerator, so that you can test at different temperatures without
ruining food in the refrigerator.

HOW TO DO COLD-WEATHER TESTING

Use the "Cold-Weather Test Logbook" on page 219. Make a couple of
copies to start with, and label the jars with "Sample" numbers so
you'll know what's in them. Then start mixing up your test batches.
Start with Sample 1 and add the desired blend (for example, B50
plus double the normal amount of your favorite additive). Continue
to make up more samples like this. I suggest that you test B50 with
all your different additives, and then test B35 with the same, and
maybe test B100 with additives only. Also, do one sample of B100
with no additives, to use as a control batch.

Put the samples in a refrigerator, along with a thermometer so
that you know what temperature the refrigerator is at. After about 8
hours or so, check on them and make notes of your results. In the
temperature column, there are 4 slots for each sample. Test them at
varying temperatures—say, 32°, 22°, 12°, and 0°F, or whatever you're
likely to encounter. Start at the warmer temperatures and work
down toward the colder ones. Just write each temperature in a slot,
along with the results to the right.

Tip: If you set the samples in a refrigerator, be sure to put them
in a leakproof plastic box with a lid, such as a storage box.
Reason: They'll likely leak some, and you don't want to
contaminate your refrigerator. While biodiesel doesn't smell
much, the antigel additives and diesel in the biodiesel smell
pretty bad.

As you make the refrigerator colder you'll see the B100 begin to
get cloudy on the bottom, or get cloudy all the way through, or

become solid halfway through and liquid halfway. Once the fuel starts looking mostly cloudy, or is very thick and appears that it wouldn't flow very well, you've reached your lowest operating temperature for that sample. Basically, you're looking for the sample that endures the coldest temperature before reaching this point. That will be your ideal winterized fuel blend.

I have an old, small refrigerator in which I did all my testing. I basically found that I achieved the best results with B50 and 4x the recommended amount of additive. I'll discuss additives more in Chapter 12.

TESTING FOR SOAP

If you research testing for soap on the Internet, you'll find several home tests you can do. Some of the tests for soap are very difficult to do and nearly impossible to understand without a chemistry background. A simple test is to visually inspect the biodiesel. If there's a gelatinous middle layer that is whitish in color, between the biodiesel and the glycerine, it will likely be soap. If your biodiesel emulsified when you started washing it, you probably have excess soap. The good news is that with enough washing, you can wash the soap out. Generally, if you process oil that titrated over 3, or that contained excess water, you'll have more soap than with a better oil. The secret to avoiding emulsions is to be *gentle*, as if washing dainty lingerie. Gently mist wash, maybe twice on bad oil, then *gently* add the water for bubble washing. Also, keep washing times to a minimum on bad oils, because that way there's much less chance that you'll have an emulsion.

EMULSIFICATION TEST

To try to *predict* washing problems and to get an idea of how much soap may be in your fuel, do an emulsification test. I recommend this test for the first few batches you make, as it could help you avoid possible emulsion problems.

To do this test, start by filling a Mason jar about 40 percent with biodiesel that has been reacted, then drained of glycerine, but not washed. Then fill it another 40 percent with water and replace the lid tightly. Now shake vigorously until the mixture emulsifies completely.

Next, observe how long it takes for the biodiesel to separate from the water. As a guide, already *washed* fuel will separate in about 10 minutes whereas poor-quality fuel, which has not been washed and contains excess soap, won't separate at all. Even fuel that's low-quality, but usable, can take several hours to separate. As long as the fuel/water mixture separates in about 3 to 5 hours, you're likely to not have problems with washing. However, if it takes more than that, I would use the shortest, gentlest methods when washing to avoid having an emulsion.

Fuel that's high in soaps or monoglycerides or diglycerides may refuse to separate even after 12 to 24 hours. If this happens, you may want to take extra precautions when proceeding further. When washing, shorten the time to 1 hour for the first wash, and add the water extra-gently. When you start bubble washing, make sure the bubbles come out slowly and gently, and keep the times short. You might even want to let the fuel settle for a week or more, draining the glycerine off the bottom every day. This allows more contaminants to settle out before you start washing and permits more methanol to evaporate from the biodiesel.

When finished separating, there should be a layer of milky water on the bottom and a layer of hazy amber biodiesel on top. You may end up with a thin middle layer also, but we won't worry about that for this test.

This test is only a rough predictor of possible wash problems. It gives an *idea* of the amount of catalyst, soaps, monoglycerides, and diglycerides that are in the fuel. It's not meant to give a quantitative measurement of the amount of any of these contaminants, but instead is an indicator of possible problems when washing the fuel.

You can do this test on washed fuel as well. If it too takes a long time to settle out, you may still have soap, monoglycerides, or diglycerides present. Fully reacted, washed biodiesel will usually separate in 10 to 30 minutes.

JAN WARNQVIST'S CONVERSION TEST

This test comes from the discussion of the test at the "Biodiesel and SVO Discussion" forums at *http://biodiesel.infopop.cc/eve/forums/a/tpc/f/9411061471/m/8281092351.*

This is considered a quick pass/fail conversion test for washed biodiesel. This test is said to be effective because biodiesel will dissolve in methanol, while triglycerides won't. It works not only with washed and dried biodiesel, but also with unwashed biodiesel that has plenty of time to settle (say, over 48 hours).

EQUIPMENT NEEDED
— A way to measure out 27 ml of methanol
— A small container with a good lid to put the 27 ml of methanol in
— A 3 ml syringe
— The biodiesel sample you wish to test

THE PROCEDURE
1 Ensure that the container is very clean and dry.
2 Add 27 ml of methanol at about 72°F into the container.
3 Use the syringe to add exactly 3 ml of the biodiesel sample (also at room-temperature) into the methanol.
4 Put the top on the container.
5 Shake the container well for about 5 seconds.

If the biodiesel completely dissolves in the methanol and you see no oil settle out on the bottom of the container, you likely have very-high-conversion biodiesel.

Generally, if oil settles out, this is sufficient as a test. It has been found by others that if no oil precipitates out, then the odds are good that the fuel meets ASTM specs for bound glycerine (mono- and digylcerides). However, if there is precipitation, this test shows that you're highly unlikely to meet ASTM specifications for bound glycerine.

Visit the *http://biodiesel.infopop.cc* website for much more discussion on this subject.

TROUBLESHOOTING YOUR PROCESSES AND RESULTS

You have at your disposal a number of ways to troubleshoot problems, analyze results that went astray, and do some detective work to figure out what went wrong with a batch of fuel. Before you try to fix any problem you're having, first attempt to identify what it is. A good way to start is to categorize what it looks like—the good old "What the heck is *that?*" test.

WHAT YOU ARE SEEING

Normal—Biodiesel that's normal can vary a great deal in appearance, depending on what you're making it from. It can range from dark amber colored to virtually colorless. When finished (including the drying), all biodiesel should be clear enough to read newsprint through, and it should be *much* thinner than the original oil. It should have a light but pleasant odor and contain no visible contaminants.

Before it has been washed, the fuel will appear slightly darker and cloudier. If you try to look through it, it will be quite hazy. Once washed, but not dried, it may appear even hazier, due to the suspended water in it.

Emulsions—A creamy, pale yellow, and mayonnaise-looking mixture. This can be a kind of swirled layer; a flat, solid layer; or all the way through. See photo on the next page. It's much easier to see in color, so I've posted color photos on our website.

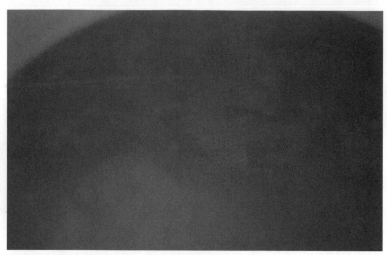

EMULSION EXAMPLE

Glop—This is a thick, gel-like failure. It usually won't flow at all, and looks like very thick pudding or jelly.

Unreacted oil—If the oil failed to react, or just barely reacted, here's what you'll see: no discernible separation layer of glycerine and biodiesel, or perhaps a very small layer (much less than the volume of the methanol you put in).

Hazy, cloudy appearance—This is most likely caused by suspended water in the fuel. If you haven't dried it yet, follow the instructions in Chapter 7. If you went through the drying process, you may not have completed it, especially in a humid environment. Or you may have introduced new moisture to the tank. See the drying section for more information. See the section in Chapter 7 for more photos and information on drying your fuel.

EMULSIONS

Definition—An emulsion is a problem that occurs when certain impurities, such as soaps, glycerine, and methanol, along with some form of overly vigorous agitation, cause the biodiesel, soap, and water to combine to form a creamy, mayonnaise-looking mess. The residual methanol is also involved here, as it helps cause these ingredients to form together. If you remove the methanol before washing, you'll reduce the chance of emulsifying.

Emulsions prevent the water and biodiesel from separating easily. It usually takes quite a bit of work to "break" an emulsion. Think of the problem like this: Normally, if you mix oil and water and stir it vigorously (as if starting on a salad dressing), they'll separate out fairly quickly when left standing. But if you add soap to the mixture and shake it, you'll emulsify the mixture, and it will take days for the ingredients to settle back out.

Emulsions can occur in several forms. If you look into your wash tank and the emulsion spans from top to bottom, it's totally emulsified (which is the worst case). Or it could just have a stubborn, emulsified middle layer in between the biodiesel and the water layer. This middle layer of emulsion can be several inches thick, or more.

Tip: Just because fuel goes from, say, an amber color to an orange when you mist wash, it doesn't mean it's emulsified. This color change is simply a result of suspended water in the fuel, which you remove later. See photo on page 102 for an example of how biodiesel changes appearance through the different stages of processing.

Cause—The most common cause of emulsification is excess soap in the wash tank when you begin your water washing and overly aggressive washing. The water stirs up the soap, then you add some agitation from either adding the water or turning on the bubbler, and you end up with an emulsion.

Excess agitation alone can also cause it. This might come from adding the water too vigorously or too long, or from bubbling too fast or with too large a bubble. Most freshly made biodiesel will contain some residual soap anyway, and excess agitation can cause that soap to bond with the water and biodiesel, putting everything in suspension together and forming an emulsion.

Lower-quality biodiesel will contain so much soap that it can emulsify merely from the bubble washing.

Prevention—If you use the same tank to process the biodiesel and then to wash it, make sure you drain *all* the glycerine out of the tank. You might have to sacrifice a little biodiesel to do this (just put that amount in your long-term settling tank to recover later), but you'll be safer. Also, if using lye, do your first draining of the glycerine after about 3 to 4 hours. Then drain every 3 to 8 hours so that the glycerine doesn't have time to begin hardening. (This is exactly what happened to us when we had one particular emulsion. Plus, we added the water a bit too vigorously and bubbled it too vigorously. Lesson learned!)

Make sure you mist wash first, then throw that water out. If it came out really saturated looking, you might want to repeat until it appears more milky white. Simply misting and then draining helps clear out the remaining soap and glycerine, especially if you have a cone bottom tank. Since misting is gentler, misting several times on high titrating oil is a good idea.

When you're done with mist washing and have disposed of the water, begin the bubble wash. After adding the water and starting the air pump, you might want to slow the air amount down a little by adjusting the air pump (if you have the adjustable kind) or by pinching the line a little, or by other means. This reduces the amount of agitation, which helps reduce the chance of an emulsion. Also, make sure your air stone isn't disintegrating, which would cause larger air bubbles and more agitation.

Shorter washing times help reduce emulsions. Again, if you know that your oil may have had more water than it should, or it titrated high, bubble wash for shorter periods and work up to longer periods, more slowly than usual. As you bubble wash, the wash water will become more and more saturated. If you bubble too long, you'll send highly saturated soapy bubbles up through the biodiesel, which in turn emulsifies the fuel.

Your goal: To make high-quality biodiesel using better oils, with complete reactions, and therefore little soap. Way to achieve your goal: Use better oils with lower FFAs and less water, do your titration carefully, measure accurately, and dewater well—all of which will help you minimize problems.

Tip: If your oil is titrating high but you really want to use it anyway, here's a pointer. You can dilute it with good oil to lower the acid number. Or you could add some biodiesel back into this batch, which effectively does the same thing. We have a dedicated settling tank into which we pour the wash water containing biodiesel. We also pour any middle-layer emulsions into it. Since the tank is cone bottomed, the water and glycerine settle out and we can separate the biodiesel. We usually just put it—like an orphan—in the next batch for reprocessing. Sometimes we save it to use with high-titrating oil to lower the overall acid number.

Cure—If you only have the middle layer emulsion and are in a hurry to finish the biodiesel, just drain away the emulsion layer. Then let that sit for several days to break on its own. After draining, you can continue to wash the biodiesel as normal.

If you've ended up with a complete emulsion, it will look like a total mess. But it usually can be "broken," so don't despair. Here are several suggestions to break emulsions, in order of effectiveness:

— Add more glycerine
— Allow more time
— Use gentle heat
— Add salt
— Add acid

ADDING MORE GLYCERINE

This method might sound crazy, but crazy like a fox. Discovered by Jack Jones, of Riverstone Biodiesel (*www.riverstonesBiodiesel. com*), it has proven to be a fairly quick way of breaking an emulsion. Usually this method is all you need, so always keep about 10 gallons of glycerine available (with the methanol still in it).

Here's how Jones describes this method (paraphrased).

To break a full emulsion, *add small amounts of the glycerine* to determine how much is really needed to break the emulsion. *It's important that you not mix these solvents too aggressively*, otherwise their emulsion-breaking power will be halted by the emulsion creating power of the soap that's present. A thorough mixing is all that's needed. It's also important to have the mixture a little warm at this point. If you can, heat the mixture up to 90°F (see Tip box for ideas).

Tip: To heat the biodiesel or the glycerine, you might use an aquarium heater. Or siphon in buckets of hot, 130°F water to help heat it up. Add the water slowly, spreading it all over the emulsion to help heat it. Then just drain the water after it sits for about 10 minutes or so. Or warm the room to 90°F for a day, which should warm the biodiesel.

HERE ARE THE STEPS
— Heat the mixture to about 90°F if possible.

— Begin adding leftover glycerine, *with the methanol still in it*, about 5 percent at a time and stir gently. (*Note*: You might need to heat the glycerine up, too. It would be best if it were warm, plus it would be more liquid that way. But be careful, it still has methanol in it.)

— If this doesn't break the emulsion, repeat the process several more times, adding up to 30 to 40 percent glycerine (that is, for a 20-gallon batch, up to 6 to 8 gallons of glycerine).

— Once the emulsion breaks, the color will return to normal (usually taking on a darker amber color, and the glycerine will settle out. Let it settle for an hour or so, then drain the glycerine out and continue washing as normal.

TIME

To fix a severe emulsion, you could simply wait it out. Often an emulsion will settle out on its own in a few days to a week or more. Some people drain the emulsion out into separate tanks or buckets and let it sit. Then when it breaks, they pump it back into the wash tank and continue washing. I've waited for 2 to 3 days for an emulsion to break, with no luck, so you might have to be very patient to use this method.

If you don't happen to have any glycerine available, you can try the hot water method, next.

HOT WATER METHOD

Start by getting approximately 4 gallons of hot water (about 120 to 130°F) and placing it higher than the tank. Using a small (½") vinyl hose, siphon the water into the tank until the bucket is empty (or pump it in with a small, fountain-type pump). Then stir very gently for several minutes. Let the water settle a few minutes, then drain the water and repeat the process several more times until the emulsion breaks. I've used this method and it does work, but it's time-consuming. I have lost a few gallons of biodiesel but saved most of it.

SALT METHOD

Salting is another method that has been used to break a severe emulsion, though I recommend that you try the other methods first. Adding salt is adding a toxic substance, which is a consideration if you dump it on the ground near plants. Also, salt accelerates the

corrosion of metals. You should be sure to wash out all the salt
before you use the biodiesel. This will cause you to use more water
washes to clear the salt out.

This method works this way: The water and the salt molecules
have more of an attraction for each other than do the water and
soap. The water will drop the soap molecules and take on the salt
molecules instead. With less soap in the water, the biodiesel will
come out of emulsion easier.

ACID METHOD

A final method is acid. I won't discuss that here, however, since it
has definite drawbacks and severe safety concerns. You should be
able to break an emulsion with the other methods above.

GLOP

Definition—Glop is a failed batch of biodiesel that results in a thick-
gel, soapy kind of substance that's definitely *not* biodiesel. You'll know
if you ever make it, as it's very thick and entirely obvious. Just don't
confuse it with emulsions, as glop is much thicker. The appearance can
vary, but it usually looks something like jelly. See photo below.

Cause—Glop is caused by excess water in your oil, or by too much
catalyst. It can also be caused by simple miscalculations, or
inaccurate titrations (human error), or using inaccurate scales when
measuring the catalyst for the titrant. The very first minibatch I
ever made turned to glop, even though I used new oil. I determined
it was due to my using a scale that
was accurate only to 1 g. Since I
was measuring 1 g, I could be off
by 100 percent or more, and in
fact I was. I then bought a more
accurate scale, redid the minibatch, and it worked perfectly.
Glop can also be caused by not
testing for water before making a
batch, or possibly by having other
unknowns in your oil (such as

GLOP (PHOTO COURTESY GRAYDON
BLAIR, UTAH BIODIESEL SUPPLY)

cleaning fluids and the like). All the more reason to know your oil source.

Prevention

— Do your titration tests several times on oil that's warm and that has been *well mixed*, to avoid testing the cream on the top of the barrel.

— *Carefully* weigh your catalyst for the titrant, using a scale accurate to 0.1 g or better.

— Make sure your calculations are accurate, for the amount of catalyst. Do the math twice, or double check your figures if using a chart or spreadsheet program to calculate the amounts.

— Test your oil for water *before* making a batch.

— *Thoroughly dewater* your oil, if using used oil, before making a batch. (All used oil should be dewatered using the methods outlined in Chapter 7.)

— Don't try to process oil that's too high in FFAs. You'll know this if it titrates at more than 4 or 5 ml. You can process oil that titrates at levels like 7 or 8 with a single-stage transesterification (I've done it several times with no problems), but I guarantee there will be an abundance of mono- and diglycerides, and therefore bound glycerine, with this type of oil. So if you do process oil this poor, do so rarely, and carefully. There's an esterification method of making biodiesel from high-titrating oil, but it's an extra process in itself and is fairly complicated and more expensive, so is not recommended until you've gained significant experience making biodiesel using good oil with the transesterification method. If you wish to learn more about the esterification method, just search for the term on the Internet.

Cure—There's no cure for glop and likely never will be, as it is no longer even oil or fuel. Consider it a failed batch, and dispose of it accordingly. If you have a sealed, Appleseed-type reactor, you may have to heat the mixture slightly to get it out. If you do this, be careful, as this can be dangerous. Heat it a little at a time until it will come out. Cone bottom reactors are easier to clean out, but can still be very difficult.

MONOGLYCERIDES AND DIGLYCERIDES

Definition—Monoglycerides and diglycerides both result from an incomplete reaction of your biodiesel. A monoglyceride is an oil molecule with two of the three fatty acid molecules broken off and the glycerine molecule still attached. A diglyceride is the same thing, but with only one of the three fatty acid molecules broken off. Neither glyceride can be seen by the naked eye, neither washes out in the washing process, and both can play a part in emulsifying your biodiesel and wash water. When burned in your engine, these two items can cause problems such as injector clogging, valve coking, poor emissions, and corrosion of some metals. They'll likely take some time to cause problems, but will eventually cause you engine trouble.

Cause—Monoglycerides and diglycerides are left after insufficient agitation, improper temperature, not enough methanol or catalyst, or using oil that titrates too high. Having excess water in the fuel could also cause problems, since the resulting soap can interfere with the reaction.

Solution—Be more precise in your catalyst measurements, both when measuring out for a reference solution and when measuring for a large batch. Make sure you agitate the mixture long enough. This is a good reason to agitate it for about 30 minutes or more longer than you think you need to. Your pump must sufficiently agitate the whole mixture, keeping everything in suspension. Be

UNDESIRABLE COMPONENTS IN BIODIESEL
This illustration shows a simple diagram of the undesirable mono- and diglycerides that can result from an incomplete reaction.

Monoglyceride showing 1 remaining fatty acid attached to the glycerine

Diglyceride showing 2 remaining fatty acids attached to the glycerine

UNDESIRABLE MONO- AND DIGLYCERIDES

sure the oil is at about 120° to 130°F *during the entire reaction process*, not just before. Monitor the temperature of the mixture when the pump is running as an indicator. Don't heat it past 148°F or you may boil off some methanol, resulting in an incomplete reaction. Use the 22 percent methanol figure to ensure that you're using enough. Some sources may convince you to use less to save money, but this amount helps ensure a complete reaction, keeping the equilibrium of the process shifted in the right direction, and is better than too little. This is all according to the University of Idaho's article on homebrew procedures. (See Resources for a link to that article.) Also, it's very important to dewater your used oil before processing it, as all used oil has water in it.

Cure—Reprocess a test batch to see whether any more glycerine drops out. See Chapter 9 for information on how to do a reprocess test.

If you do a reprocess test and find you had an incomplete reaction (highly likely in this case), your only real option is to either use it as is and take your chances, or dilute it either with better-quality B100 or with petrodiesel.

Or, you can *reprocess the whole batch*. I've never had a totally failed batch like this, so I've never had to do a reprocess. To reprocess a full batch you'll have to use a smaller amount of methanol and catalyst than the first time. Since there's no way to know how far the reaction went, trying to reprocess is mostly experimental on your part. Basically, start by reprocessing the failed batch a liter at a time. Just experiment with using smaller ratios of methanol, starting at about 3.5 percent, and increase that percentage for each successive minibatch. Use roughly 1 g of catalyst per liter (since I'm recommending a liter jug) in the test. Then just make some minibatches, each time increasing the amount of methanol until you've made 4 or 5 minibatches; if it doesn't eventually work out, start again. This time go back to the minimal amount of methanol, but increase the catalyst to 2 g per liter and make a batch. If *that* fails, increase the methanol again, but not the catalyst. Just continue until you get the desired separation, and do some math to determine the amount to use in your full-sized batch.

This can be expensive and time-consuming, however. Usually, running an occasional tank of fuel that's only slightly out of spec won't harm an engine, though this isn't guaranteed. Running it on a consistent basis is pretty much sure to cause you grief at some point, so don't take shortcuts.

NO SEPARATION

Definition—This is another problem I've never had, but will describe in case you do. This condition is characterized by no distinct visual separation of the biodiesel and glycerine. If you ran the whole process, and you let it settle for 8 hours or more, but still don't see that distinct layer of glycerine and biodiesel, you have a problem.

Cause—This condition generally indicates that you didn't use enough catalyst, methanol, agitation, agitation time, or heat. If any one of these items is sufficiently lacking due to a miscalculation or other cause, you could end up with no separation layer or a very small one. Generally you have to mess up really badly to have this happen.

Solution—In the future, take more care with your calculations. You should review how to do them accurately, to ensure that you haven't adopted a faulty method or done something else not to the plan or recipe. Otherwise, review everything, from your oil to heating and so on, to find what you did wrong. This is a good reason to always do a minibatch on a new oil source. If you can process such a batch successfully, chances are good that you'll be able to make larger batches as well.

Cure—Do a reprocess test. See Chapter 9 for information on how to do such a test. If you get the separation this time, your calculations were off. If you must reprocess, see the cure for monoglycerides on page 190 for more information on reprocessing a whole batch.

SOAP

Definition—Soap is a byproduct of the biodiesel-making process. It's often seen as a gelatin-like, whitish layer that forms between the biodiesel and the glycerine. It can also appear as a foamy layer on top of the fuel.

SOME SOAPY BUBBLES ARE NORMAL WHEN MAKING BIODIESEL

Cause—Soap is caused by excess catalyst, water in the oil, or poor-quality oil. It's fairly common to see soap in the fuel, since the entire process of making biodiesel produces soap as a byproduct. Soap is mainly a concern if it causes problems like emulsions, or if you can't seem to wash it out of your fuel. Seeing signs of soap in the early stages of making biodiesel is no cause for alarm.

Solution—Be careful with your titration and your calculations. If you think you did all that accurately, you might want to make up another batch of reference solution and try a minibatch again. My first batch of reference solution wasn't accurate enough, which caused my calculations to be off, which in turn caused my first minibatch to end up as glop. Accuracy is important. You should also choose better, drier oil, with fewer FFAs, and should dewater your oil thoroughly before processing it.

Cure—Do a mist water wash to remove the soap contaminants. If you think you have very soapy biodiesel, you may have to do more mist water washes before moving on to bubble washing. Then when starting the bubble washes, be very gentle when adding the water and with the bubbling itself. You might limit your first bubble wash to 1 hour, then drain and start again.

ABRASIVE SOLIDS

Definition—Some abrasive solids appear in almost all biodiesel made from used oil. Of course, solids like this can accelerate wear on injectors, fuel pumps, and other engine parts. You want to do your best to remove them.

Cause—Small solids (invisible to the naked eye) are normal in finished biodiesel, but must be removed.

Cure—Wash the fuel well, and filter the final product down to 5 or 10 microns. Note that most filters are rated nominally, meaning they only catch a percentage (often scarcely 50 percent) of the particles in that range. Therefore, if you suspect high levels of contaminants, or want to be extra careful about contaminants in your fuel, you should filter the fuel by using a high-quality fuel filter that's rated at a higher efficiency in the desired micron rating. You can do this by selecting a filter with an absolute micron rating, meaning it will remove a much higher percentage of the particulates it's rated at. Settling the fuel for a few days and not pumping off the bottom 3 inches from the fuel storage tank may also help, because some of the particles may settle out.

HIGH FFA LEVELS

Definition—High FFA fuel is biodiesel that has an FFA content higher than ASTM standards allow. If you send your fuel out to be tested, you could find out that it has a high FFA content and doesn't meet ASTM standards. Fuel with a high FFA content usually has a high acid content, possibly causing stability issues and sludge buildup inside fuel lines and components.

Cause—This condition is usually caused by improper processing or inaccurate titrations. It can also be a result of fuel degradation caused by long-term storage, storage in the sun for long periods, or bacteria or water in the fuel.

Solution—Ensure that you dry the fuel properly. Make sure your titration measurements are accurate. Don't store the biodiesel for longer than 3 to 4 months, and add a biocide to the fuel. Try not to store the fuel in the direct sun for long periods. Make sure the storage container is well sealed and full, thus minimizing exposure to the air, which can contain moisture that could accelerate bacteria growth.

Cure—You could try a reprocess test to see whether the fuel reacted completely in the first place. This could help rule out inaccurate titrations. See Chapter 9 for information on how to do such a test.

If you've read all the above, you've likely noticed a pattern. Most problems are often traceable to the same areas, such as proper oil selection, dewatering, proper heating, agitation, processing time, washing, drying, filtering, and so on. So it should be clear by now that cutting corners, using inferior equipment, or trying to make biodiesel improperly *will* result in fuel problems and engine problems.

CHAPTER 11

STORING AND DISPENSING BIODIESEL

The general rule is that biodiesel can be stored for up to six months, either in steel or plastic (MDPE) drums or in totes of a desired size. The actual length of time depends on many factors, such as your feedstock; how well the fuel has been processed, washed, and dried; and where you store it, how, and in what type of container. Maintenance of the storage tanks and other factors can determine the storage life of biodiesel. Additives are available to extend the storage life of biodiesel if needed. If you'll be storing it for some time, you want to keep it out of direct sunlight, to avoid deterioration of the fuel. Also be aware that biodiesel can absorb moisture while in storage. To minimize this, store it in well-sealed containers, or indoors, and try not to leave any airspace in the storage container.

Biodiesel is very hard to ignite (about *twice* as difficult as petrodiesel), so it's fairly safe to store around ignition sources such as light switches, motors, and the like. I've even tried to ignite it with a torch and couldn't get it to burn by itself. Still, just to be on the safe side, you shouldn't store it near flames or sparks such as those from a grinder. Use common sense here.

If storing large amounts of fuel for fleet use, you should consider adding a biocide (a fuel treatment that kills bacteria in fuel) periodically to prevent any possible bacterial growth. This is more of a concern with biodiesel versus petrodiesel, due to the fact that biodiesel can hold about 1,500 ppm of water (as compared with petrodiesel, at about 50 ppm of water).

You may want to do a shock treatment by using the biocide on all fleet vehicles and fuel storage tanks before their first use of the fuel. This wards off problems, as most fuel tanks contain some moisture, and since adding "neat" (B100) biodiesel can accelerate any bacterial growth already in the tanks.

Dispensing the biodiesel can be done in a number of ways. Here are several ideas.

—Buy a high-quality electric pump such as those sold by Tuthill Fill-Rite. These have a regular fuel nozzle and everything you need. The drawback is that they're a bit expensive, running over $200 for a nonbiodiesel compatible model and closer to $400 for one that's listed as biodiesel compatible. It's best to look for one that's biodiesel compatible, since not all are. But I should point out that our first Fill-Rite pump is still going strong today after over 1,500 gallons of B100, and it's not even considered "biodiesel compatible" as that option wasn't available when we bought ours. The fuel hose did soften after about 1,000 gallons, so we replaced it with a biodiesel-compatible hose and have had no further problems. If you do have an older, nonbiodiesel-compatible pump,

BE SURE TO GET BIODIESEL-COMPATIBLE PUMPS AND HOSES

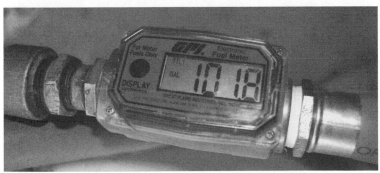

YOU CAN PUT A FUEL METER ON THE PUMP NOZZLE IF NEEDED

I believe you can buy the parts to convert it to biodiesel-compatible, to avoid having to buy a new pump.

— Buy an inexpensive barrel pump from a company like Harbor Freight. These might not hold up as long as a high-quality pump, yet replacing them is both cheap and simple. With such a pump, you can simply pump right into a dedicated 5-gallon gas can (clearly labeled for only biodiesel) and transfer it to your vehicle. Or you can put a longer hose on it and pump straight into your vehicle. This type is a little slow but gets the job done.

— Buy a higher-quality hand pump, which might last somewhat longer and be a little faster too. Note that some hand pumps are

OUR BIODIESEL FILLING STATION,
WITH ITS FILL-RITE PUMP

really slow. If you don't have patience or strong arms, be aware of the flow rating when you're shopping.

— You can even use your processor's pump to fill 5-gallon biodiesel cans. I've done that a few times, but watch it carefully, as even the cheap pumps will fill 5 gallons pretty quickly. The processor pump can even dispense directly into your vehicle's tank, but you definitely want a fuel nozzle on the end to shut it off when the tank gets full.

— Or, if you pump your biodiesel up into a tank that's high enough off the ground (something like those seen on farms resting on stands), gravity will do the rest when it's time to fill up.

IMPROVING YOUR FUEL'S COLD-WEATHER PERFORMANCE

Biodiesel has an inherently higher *cloud point* than does petrodiesel. Cloud point is defined as the temperature at which waxy solids first appear during the cooling of diesel fuel. It's a quality-control test that has been in use by petroleum refineries for well over 50 years.

Biodiesel will begin to develop cloudiness from around the low 20s to the mid-40s Fahrenheit, compared to diesel, which averages 15°F (nonwinterized). Winterized diesel, which is usually merely a combination of No. 1 and No. 2 diesel, can go down much lower without clouding; how low depends on the blend, which varies by region. In wintertime, petroleum refineries supply seasonally adjusted diesel fuels to various regions of North America. Due to the diverse climatic requirements, they must satisfy over one hundred temperature zones (another reason for the high cost of regular fuel).

In blending, it's useful to know that No. 1 diesel is a refinery stock that's similar to kerosene and jet fuel. It has excellent winter operability because the cloud point is extremely low, typically in the range of –40°F. However, it has several drawbacks. It has a lower energy content, which affects the fuel's economy and power. In addition, its lubricity is generally poorer than that of No. 2 diesel, and the price is typically higher.

It's recommended that the fuel cloud point be colder (6°F colder is often quoted) than the lowest anticipated ambient temperature at which the vehicle is expected to operate. Otherwise, there's a significant risk of filter plugging and downtime.

WAYS TO IMPROVE COLD-WEATHER PERFORMANCE OF BIODIESEL

Blend it with petrodiesel. Yes, I hate doing that also, but it does work well. Blends of between B35 and B60 seem to work best. If you're in a *really cold* area, you might even need to go to a B20. Do some experimenting and testing, as described in Chapter 9. But just for a guideline, here's what we do: When we feel that temperatures will drop to below 45°F for several hours, we run a B60 blend. When it will drop below 35°F, we run a B50; below 25°F, a B35; and below 15°F we would go to B20. We've never had a gelling or a starting problem in any of our three diesels using these guidelines. High-quality fuel helps here, as low-grade fuel, with its excess glycerine, will likely gel at higher temperatures.

Blend your biodiesel with antigel additives. A few additives on the market claim they're made for biodiesel. But I think that most manufacturers have yet to develop a *true* biodiesel additive that will lower the cloud point of B100 sufficiently. The additives that work well in petrodiesel do little in biodiesel, I've found. My tests have been discouraging with B100, but they work fairly well with B50. The way these seem to function is that they actually work to lower the cloud point of the petrodiesel, which in turn lowers the overall cloud point of the blended fuel. The popular additives are:

— **Power Service Arctic Express Biodiesel Antigel**—This is the one brand that most homebrew biodiesel makers swear by. They all say that it doesn't work very well on B100, but works fine with B50 or so. It's similar to the product on page 98.

— **Primrose 4033 Biodiesel Winter fuel additive**—The manufacturer claims this to be a biodiesel-specific additive. I've tested this and it works fine, but only with B50 or so. Maybe it was my particular biodiesel, but I think it and all other additives need more work.

To buy these products, search the Internet for the names above, and you'll find the dealers.

Winterize Your Fuel—Information on the USDA website reports a new technique that can dramatically lower the cloud point of biodiesel. It involves a three-step winterization process of mixing in additives, chilling the fuel, and filtering out the solids. Their researchers have produced biodiesel fuels capable of starting engines at temperatures as low as 5°F, making them comparable to petroleum-based diesel fuels.

There are some drawbacks to this method as it's said that this "winterized" fuel will have a lower cetane rating than normal. Lower cetane numbers can result in increased harmful exhaust emissions, especially nitrogen oxides. The other downside to this method is that the long-term stability is decreased for those who might store it for long periods. Still, the technique has some promise to it.

ANOTHER NEW IDEA FOR WINTERIZING

This is one of the newest and most promising ideas out there. This idea comes from the biodiesel and SVO (straight vegetable oil) discussion forums at: *http://Biodiesel.infopop.cc/groupee/forums/a/tpc/f/419605551/m/9441081511.*[66]

A forum member has posted the following information, which looks to be a highly promising way of pretreating your waste oil to substantially lower the biodiesel's cloud point.

Here's how: When making biodiesel from waste oils, there's a technique that involves removing as much of the tallows as possible before making the fuel. (Nothing new there.... But this method may be.)

Take a 55-gallon, open head barrel, and fill it about 80 percent full of your waste oil (minimizing the water and crud when filling).

Then add 10 to 15 percent glycerine (straight from a previous reaction, with the methanol still in it), and stir the whole batch up for a few minutes. You don't need to be overly aggressive with the mixing; just give it a good stir. It's said to work better if it's not really mixed too aggressively.

Finally, let it stand for around for 2 to 3 days undisturbed. After that you can draw off the liquid oil, starting from the top. It may be a little cloudy at this point, but will soon clarify as you heat and dewater it.

You'll find that the remaining tallows in your oil will have settled to the bottom of the barrel and become much whiter and thicker than usual. These will tend to stay put when you draw off the oil.

The glycerine will settle out in the tallow layer where they seem to make the bottom layer stickier than usual.

Then process the oil as normal, and your biodiesel will have a much lower gel point (cold filter plugging point) than it would have if you had used the oil without pretreating as above.

It has been confirmed by laboratory testing that the CFPP of biodiesel made using this process is 14°F , before any additives are used.

HEATERS

A final note is that you can also install all kinds of heaters on your vehicle. You'll need to heat the entire fuel system for this to work, otherwise the unheated section could gel solid and you still won't be able to drive the vehicle. There are fuel tank heaters, inline heaters, block heaters, and so on. Do a search on the Internet for the terms "Racor diesel fuel heaters," "Fox diesel heaters," or just "diesel fuel heaters." But also note that this can get expensive. The factory block heater in my truck, for example, uses 1,000 watts, so operational costs can mount fairly quickly, not to mention the cost of the equipment. But if you can run B100 all year long, it will likely pay for itself in less than a year.

STARTING A BIODIESEL COOPERATIVE

If you have friends who also own and run diesels, you might want to consider starting a biodiesel cooperative. Basically, a cooperative is a group of people joining together to make biodiesel. Their association provides several advantages. Members (like you) can afford to purchase a better processor with their combined money. These extra funds could allow you to invest in nicer fuel pumps, meters, methanol recovery systems, solar preheaters, and other desirable equipment and add-ons. You can divide up the work of collecting the oil, making the biodiesel, and performing other tasks. One of you might have a better location (say, in a nearby suburb)

WE NO LONGER HAVE TO GIVE ALL OUR MONEY TO POLLUTING REFINERIES

than do others in the co-op. You'll usually incur much less individual startup expense out-of-pocket, because you're sharing some or all of the costs. Furthermore, you can put your combined knowledge to work to research solutions to problems, create new or better ways of doing things, jerry-rig a work-around when someone bumps up against an obstacle, and so forth. Everyone benefits.

How you set up your cooperative is entirely the decision of you and your group. Here are a few ideas to get you thinking about it. You could charge everyone a membership fee (annual, with perhaps monthly dues to create a flow of cash) to join, especially if you personally did all the work of building the first processor. You could even make money this way. I suggest that you stipulate that a certain percentage of funds would go into an equipment account for maintenance, upgrades, and the like. Then if you yourself make all the fuel, you might charge a little more than it costs to make it, thus paying for your time.

With a metered delivery pump, you could have everyone log the amount of fuel they take from your storage tank each time. Then they could pay the cooperative monthly, or whatever you decide on.

For some good information about forming and running a biodiesel co-op, check out the Piedmont Biofuels website at *http://biofuels.coop*.

FREQUENTLY ASKED QUESTIONS

You will likely find most of your lingering questions about biodiesel—even questions that friends or family members may pose to you—answered in this FAQ section.

WHAT IS BIODIESEL?

Biodiesel is simply a very safe, ecofriendly, alternative energy fuel made from a renewable resource such as soybean, canola oil, and so on. It's made through a chemical reaction called transesterification that converts new or used oil into biodiesel plus a byproduct of glycerine. The resulting fuel has many benefits, including being much cleaner burning and possessing much higher lubricity than petrodiesel. As a bonus, it helps us to reduce our dependence on foreign oil. When made at home, it's cheaper to obtain than regular petrodiesel.

CAN I USE BIODIESEL IN MY VEHICLE?

Biodiesel can be used in any diesel engine with no modification required, unless you have natural-rubber fuel lines. If your vehicle was made from about 1993 on, you're fairly safe. Newer vehicles assembled since about the year 1993 contain synthetic fuel lines

SEMITRUCKS CAN RUN BIODIESEL AND MEET EPACT REQUIREMENTS

CERTAIN TRACTORS SHIP FROM THE FACTORY WITH B5

MY PERSONAL DIESEL TRUCK RUNS GREAT ON BIODIESEL

and are totally safe, as far as my research and experience has shown. The problems with older vehicles are that biodiesel can attack natural rubber fuel lines over time, cause leaking and other conditions. Another concern is that biodiesel can clean fuel lines and tanks so much that it can paradoxically lead to clogging of fuel filters and such. To see whether your vehicle is compatible, start by checking your fuel lines (or have a mechanic do it for you). If they're rubber, replace them with a synthetic line and you'll be fine. You should also check your owner's manual to learn whether the manufacturer specifically recommends that you not use biodiesel, for whatever reason; contact your dealer for more information. If in doubt, a blend of B20 (20 percent biodiesel and 80 percent petrodiesel) is considered safe for virtually any vehicle.

HAS BIODIESEL BEEN THOROUGHLY TESTED?

Extensive research has been done on biodiesel. Such research has included studies performed by the U.S. Department of Energy, the U.S. Department of Agriculture (USDA), Stanadyne Automotive Corp. (the largest diesel fuel injection equipment manufacturer in the U.S.), Lovelace Respiratory Research Institute, and Southwest Research Institute, as well as many others. Research into the many facets of biodiesel is ongoing. Biodiesel is the first and only alternative fuel to have completed the stringent health-effects testing requirements of the federal Clean Air Act, a mandate of the U.S. Environmental Protection Agency. Biodiesel has been proven to perform similarly to diesel in more than 50 million successful road miles in almost all types of diesel engines, including many off-road miles and countless marine hours. Currently there are hundreds of major fleets using biodiesel successfully.

WHO'S USING BIODIESEL?

Biodiesel is being used and promoted by numerous celebrities and public figures, such as Willie Nelson, Bonnie Raitt, Jay Leno, and many more. In addition, hundreds of major fleets currently use B20, including the U.S. Postal Service, the City of Philadelphia, the USDA, numerous public transit systems, national parks, school districts, private recycling and concrete companies, and the National Aeronautics and Space Administration (NASA). Many of the 50 states have mandated that within the next few years all diesel sold at the pumps will contain some percentage of biodiesel, or that a designated percentage of all diesel fuel sold will be biodiesel. Biodiesel is here to stay.

HOW IS BIODIESEL MADE?

Biodiesel is made through a process called transesterification. (See the full description in Chapter 1.)

WHAT ARE BIODIESEL'S BENEFITS?

Biodiesel stands far superior above petrodiesel in every respect, except for cold-weather performance. (See next question.) It is much safer, biodegrades more quickly if spilled, is nontoxic, burns much more cleanly, has higher lubricity, is ecofriendly, and is made from renewable resources instead of a dwindling supply of petrodiesel.

Many people would agree that making biodiesel at home for about 85 cents a gallon is their favorite benefit. And we wouldn't have to fight wars over biodiesel. See Chapter 1 for a full list of benefits.

WHAT ARE THE DRAWBACKS TO BIODIESEL?

Solvency—Biodiesel has a solvent effect that may release deposits accumulated on tank walls or pipes from previous storage of diesel fuel, so precautions should be observed when switching over to biodiesel. This applies primarily to high-mileage vehicles over 100,000 miles, or those poorly maintained. The release of these deposits may cause fuel filters to clog sooner than expected, so it's best to be prepared by carrying a spare fuel filter in the vehicle (if this applies to you).

Cold weather—Biodiesel will generally start to gel at higher temperatures than No. 2 diesel fuel, which can pose a problem if you're running B100 ("neat" biodiesel). A simple fix is to run B50 or less, which you can run seasonally in some fairly cold climates without worry. (See more details on cold-weather performance in Chapter 12.)

Nitrogen emissions—Fueling with biodiesel that hasn't been treated with additives tends to increase emissions of oxides of nitrogen, commonly known as NOx. This increase can be anywhere from 1 to 15 percent, depending on the engine type and blend of biodiesel used. NOx emissions can be reduced using additives at a rate of anywhere from 5 to 30 percent, depending on the additive and feedstock used to produce the biodiesel.

Bacteria—If you already have bacterial growth in your fuel tank, there's a *small chance* that adding biodiesel may cause the problem to accelerate. A simple and cheap solution is to run some biocide through your tanks every few months. This might cost as little as $10 per year, so it's well worth it.

IS BIODIESEL THE SAME THING AS RAW VEGETABLE OIL?

No, raw vegetable oil is much thicker than biodiesel and is totally different, chemically speaking. Biodiesel has been put through the process of transesterification, which basically breaks the oil molecules down and leaves biodiesel plus glycerine. See the definition of "transesterification" in the Glossary for more information.

Yes, biodiesel is approved for use in automobiles in the United States.

HOW DO BIODIESEL EMISSIONS COMPARE TO PETRODIESEL?
Overall, biodiesel can cause approximately a 75 to 90 percent reduction in overall emissions, compared to petrodiesel. About the only area that isn't lower are the nitrogen emissions.

HOW LONG CAN I STORE BIODIESEL?
Biodiesel can be stored for roughly the same time that petrodiesel can. Even petrodiesel has a limited storage time. If stored properly (in a dry, sealed container), biodiesel can probably be stored up to three or even six months.

WHY HAVEN'T WE BEEN WIDELY USING BIODIESEL BEFORE?
Because petrodiesel was cheaper to produce, and because fossil fuel was thought to be inexhaustible, our society has used it for our primary source of fuel. But now that biodiesel production is cost-competitive, we're seeing more of it, and it's fast becoming a popular alternative. Plus, we're realizing that we need to protect our environment, and that our oil reserves won't last forever. After years of fighting wars to protect our oil interests, we're growing weary of our foreign oil dependence and sick of fighting wars and losing American lives over oil.

HOW DOES THE COST OF BIODIESEL COMPARE TO REGULAR DIESEL?
If you make biodiesel at home, your costs will likely run 65 to 95 cents per gallon (it depends greatly on the cost of methanol and the catalyst at the time). Currently, as of October 2007 our cost is about 90 cents per gallon, though we've made it for as little as 55 cents per gallon. That makes it a lot cheaper. Commercial biodiesel, however, will run about the same price as petrodiesel, yet offers many more advantages.

HOW WILL BIODIESEL AFFECT THE POWER OF MY ENGINE?
With biodiesel, you'll have the same power as you do with petrodiesel. See the section "Benefits of Biodiesel" in Chapter 1.

IS BIODIESEL SAFE?
If it's made right, and of high quality, biodiesel is extremely safe for your engine—plus it's *much safer* than petrodiesel for the

environment. Also, in the event of a collision with another vehicle or object, biodiesel is much safer because of its higher flash point. It's also less harmful if you inadvertently splash it on you, as it's considered a nontoxic substance.

WILL BIODIESEL VOID MY VEHICLE WARRANTY?

Well, that's a complicated question. Here's the long answer, as given by the National Biodiesel Board:

"Most major engine companies have stated formally that the use of blends up to B20 will not void their parts and workmanship warranties. This includes blends below 20% Biodiesel, such as the 2% Biodiesel blends that are becoming more common. Several statements from the engine companies are available on the NBB website. Some engine companies have already specified that the Biodiesel must meet ASTM D-6751 as a condition, while others are still in the process of adopting D-6751 within their company or have their own set of guidelines for Biodiesel use that were developed prior to the approval of D-6751. It is anticipated that the entire industry will incorporate the ASTM Biodiesel standard into their owner's manuals over time.

"With Biodiesel that meets the D-6751 specification, there have been over 45 million miles of successful, problem-free, real-world operation with B20 blends in a wide variety of engines, climates, and applications. The steps taken by the Biodiesel industry to work with the engine companies and to ensure that fuel meets the newly accepted ASTM standards provides confidence to users and engine manufacturers that their Biodiesel experiences will be positive and trouble-free."

Update: According to another recent article on the National Biodiesel Board's website, Daimler Chrysler has now officially approved the use of B20 in the company's 2007 Dodge Rams. They'll also be shipping one of their new diesel-powered vehicles from the factory with B5 in it, so they're encouraging the growth of biodiesel use, as are many other vehicle and engine manufacturers. John Deere is doing the same with its tractors, provided that the B5 biodiesel is purchased from an accredited producer or distributor. Expect to see more and more manufacturers officially approving the use of biodiesel very soon, and expect the trend to accelerate as the fuel's popularity grows.

FURTHER LEARNING AND RESOURCES

CONVERSIONS

If you need to convert metric to imperial, or vice versa, here are a few useful formulas:

— 1 gallon = 3.785 liters

To convert gallons to liters, multiply by 3.785

— 1 liter = 0.264 gallons

To convert liters to gallons, divide by 3.785

— 1 ounce = 29.57 ml

To convert ounces to ml, multiply by 29.57

— 1 ml = 0.033 ounce

To convert ml to ounces, divide by 29.57

— To convert from Celsius to Fahrenheit, multiply the Celsius temperature by 1.8.

Then add 32° to adjust for the offset in the Fahrenheit scale.

— Or to convert just about anything from temperatures to distances to volume, go online to *www.onlineconversion.com*

Other helpful formulas:

— 1 cc on a syringe = 1 ml

— "cc" stands for cubic centimeters (1 cc = 0.061 cubic inch)

— "ml" stands for milliliters (one thousandth of a liter, or 0.001 liter)

Below are some websites and forums where you can learn more about biodiesel. These sites are listed on our website, and you can just click on them there.

EZ BIODIESEL—*www.ezbiodiesel.com/bookbonus.htm*
This is our informational website expressly for purchasers of this book. It contains a great collection of good information available to help homebrewers of biodiesel—some of it not available to the general public. This site has dozens of pages with links to vendors, other biodiesel websites, and retailers of processors, kits, parts, books, and accessories. In addition to the vast amount of information and many resources that this site makes available, it contains many helpful color photos relating to biodiesel.

COLLABORATIVE BIODIESEL TUTORIAL—
www.Biodieselcommunity.org/index.php

BIODIESELNOW.COM FORUMS—
http://forums.Biodieselnow.com/default.asp?CAT_ID=2
A place where others go to discuss biodiesel topics. Caution: You'll have to sift through tons of theoretical, opinionated, and sometimes downright misleading information here.

NATIONAL BIODIESEL BOARD WEBSITE—*www.Biodiesel.org*
This site contains a lot of good information. This is the official biodiesel website.

WILLIE NELSON BIODIESEL WEBSITE—*www.wnBiodiesel.com*

WIKIPEDIA—*http://en.wikipedia.org/wiki/Main_Page*
This is honestly a great reference site, offering definitions, illustrations, additional reading, and explanations of just about everything (such as feedstocks, chemicals and chemical processes, and other topics relating to the making of biodiesel).

WORLD'S FASTEST DIESEL DRAGSTER—*www.cumminsracing.com*
This vehicle hit a top speed of 167.43 miles per hour on a quarter mile dragstrip, using B100.

WHERE TO FIND BIODIESEL STATIONS IN YOUR AREA—
www.biodiesel.org/buyingbiodiesel/retailfuelingsites

"HOMEBREWING BIODIESEL" REPORT FROM THE UNIVERSITY OF IDAHO—
www.uidaho.edu/bioenergy/NewsReleases/Technote7_HB.pdf

"BIODIESEL EDUCATION" WEBSITE AT THE UNIVERSITY OF IDAHO—
www.uidaho.edu/bioenergy

FUEL QUALITY TESTING—Fuel-only tests are available at
www.ezbiodiesel.com/bookbonus.htm

ASTM D6751 FUEL TEST DESCRIPTIONS—
www.biodieseltesting.com/tests.php
Each individual test is described here—what it tests for and what that means to you.

INFORMATION ON STILLS AND METHANOL RECOVERY—
www.moonshine-still.com and *http://homedistiller.org*

WHERE TO OBTAIN YOUR CHEMICALS

You can order your chemicals from various suppliers, many of them now online.

LYE (NaOH)

Lye (sodium hydroxide) used to be commonly found as Red Devil Lye brand, and can still be found in many places. But this product has been discontinued, so it's getting harder to find. There are other sources for sodium hydroxide. Try your local chemical supply store (look under "Chemicals - Retail" or "Chemicals - Wholesale and Manufacturers" in the yellow pages of your phone book). Lye itself is discussed all throughout this book, since it has been the common catalyst used. Using KOH flakes can be easier to use, though (as discussed in the text), so you might want to use it instead of NaOH.

POTASSIUM HYDROXIDE (KOH)

This is the catalyst we currently use. As of August 2007, our price was about $59 for 32 lbs, in sealed containers.

AAA Chemicals is our current favorite place for KOH, because they sell it in 2 lb. sealed bottles, thus keeping it dry until you need it. This seller doesn't require a hazmat (hazardous materials) waiver before shipping, like many do. It can be reached at *www.aaa-chemicals.com/index.html*.

The website *www.braintan.com* sells KOH in a 20 lb. bag for approximately $45. It's 99.5 percent pure, which is just great.

Another useful website is *www.chemistrystore.com/potassium_ hydroxide.htm.*

Other sources include pool supply stores, farming stores, co-ops, and tractor supply stores. Some people have even found KOH at their hardware store. Or try your local chemical supply company, as many will sell KOH to you.

METHANOL

We currently get our methanol from the local chemical supply company. As of November 2007 our retail price is $180 for a 55-gallon barrel.

Methanol is commonly available at racetracks, sold as racing fuel. We have bought it at a local go-kart track (professional karts). You might find it at a dragstrip, a circle track, and the like.

Or call your local auto parts stores, engine builders, and hot rod shops and ask if they know where you can buy methanol. You can look on the Internet for distributors of Sunoco Race Fuels. Or try ChemCentral; you can buy its chemicals online, or nationwide in the U.S., at *www.chemcentral.com.*

Also, try your local fuel suppliers. Short of that, try chemical supply companies listed in the phone book.

GLOSSARY

ANHYDROUS—Means "without water." Transesterification of biodiesel must be an anhydrous process, otherwise funny things happen. Water in the vegetable oil causes either no reaction or cloudy biodiesel, and water in lye or methanol renders it less useful or even useless, depending on how much water is present.

BIODIESEL—An environmentally safe, low-polluting fuel made through the process of transesterification from fresh or waste vegetable oils (triglycerides). It's made commercially as well as privately, around the world.

BUBBLE WASH—A method of final washing of biodiesel through air agitation. Biodiesel floats above a quantity of water. Bubbles created by an aquarium air pump and air stone are injected into the water. Since the water bubbles are created in the water, they rise through the biodiesel as a water bubble, absorbing water-soluble impurities in the biodiesel. As the bubble reaches the surface and bursts, it then forms a small water drop, which then travels back down through the biodiesel, cleaning on the way down. This method cleans as the bubble rises, and as the water drop sinks.

CANOLA—Canola oil is a term that comes from the words "Canadian" and "oil." It's a vegetable oil derived from the rapeseed plant (member of the mustard family).

CATALYST—A catalyst is a chemical that causes the acceleration (increase in rate) of a chemical reaction. The catalyst itself isn't generally consumed by the overall reaction. For making biodiesel, either KOH or lye is used as the catalyst.

CAUSTIC—Meaning "causes corrosion," or the deterioration of a material. Sodium hydroxide, also called caustic soda, is one example. Caustic substances are *extremely* harmful to living tissue and structures.

CLOUD POINT—The temperature at which waxy solids first appear during the cooling of diesel fuel.

DELIQUESCENCE—When a substance eventually dissolves in the water that it absorbs. This property is called deliquescence. KOH and lye will absorb so much water when left exposed to the air that it will soon become a solid drop of water, due to deliquescence.

DIGLYCERIDES—This can get complicated, so to simplify it: Oil is basically a triglyceride, which is a glycerine molecule with three long-chain fatty acid molecules attached. When we process used oil into biodiesel, we want to separate the glycerine molecule from the fatty acids. The triglyceride breaks down one molecule at a time. Once one fatty acid molecule breaks away, we're left with a diglyceride ("di" meaning "two"). After breaking off one more fatty acid chain, we're left with a monoglyceride ("mono" meaning "one"). If we reach complete reaction, we break off the third fatty acid, and the glycerine now settles to the bottom. Monoglycerides and diglycerides remaining in the fuel can't be seen, but can be harmful to engines. This is all the more reason to ensure that you do all you can to process the fuel thoroughly, achieving a complete reaction. See Chapter 10 for more information.

EMULSIFICATION—To emulsify; to form an emulsion.

EMULSION—A biodiesel emulsion occurs when the methanol and soap in the biodiesel trap the wash water, forming a very cloudy substance that looks like mayonnaise mixed in with biodiesel. Emulsions can be broken. (See Chapter 10 for more information.)

ESTERS—Any of a large group of organic compounds formed when an acid and alcohol are mixed.

ETHANOL—Also known as ethyl alcohol or grain alcohol. Ethanol is a colorless, flammable, chemical compound. It can be made from sugar or starch in crops such as corn, sugar cane, switchgrass, and more. It can be used to make biodiesel, but seldom is used for that purpose, because of the higher costs as compared to methanol.

EXOTHERMIC—Describes a process or reaction that releases energy in the form of heat, usually resulting from the mixing of two chemicals. Mixing methanol and a catalyst produces heat, or an exothermic reaction.

FLASH POINT—The temperature that a fuel must reach to vaporize into a gas that can be burned. Biodiesel's flash point is around 250°F—roughly twice that of petrodiesel.

GLOP—Slang for a failed batch of biodiesel that usually results in a jelly-like tank full of oil. It can also be fairly solid. Usually caused by inaccurate lye measurements or improper titration. Also caused by oil that's too high in FFAs, water, or other substances.

GLYCERIDE—An ester formed between one or more acids and glycerol.

GLYCERINE—A byproduct of biodiesel production. It appears as a very dark and thick, oily-looking fluid. Also commonly called glycerol or glycerine, it's technically a sugar alcohol and fittingly is sweet-tasting and of low toxicity when purified. (Biodiesel glycerine is not pure straight out of the processor, so don't leave it where animals can get at it as they like the sweet taste, but the remaining catalyst and methanol could harm them.) Purified glycerine can be used to make soap and several thousand other things.

HYGROSCOPIC—The ability of a substance to absorb moisture from the air, or items around it. Both KOH and lye are highly hygroscopic.

IMMISCIBLE—A chemistry term that refers to the property of liquids that are unable to be mixed easily.

KOH—Potassium hydroxide, a chemical compound sometimes known as caustic potash, potassa, potash lye, or potassium hydrate. It is a very alkaline compound and can be used to make biodiesel.

LYE—Sodium hydroxide (NaOH), also known as lye or caustic soda, is another caustic base, very similar to KOH, used in our case to make biodiesel.

MDPE—Medium density polyethylene is a polyethylene thermoplastic made from petroleum. MDPE has more tensile strength than lower-density polyethylene. MDPE is resistant to many different solvents. By contrast, LDPE is low-density polyethylene, while HDPE is high-density polyethylene.

METHANOL—Also known as methyl alcohol, carbinol, wood alcohol, wood naptha, or wood spirits. Methanol is most often made from the methane component in natural gas. Methanol can also be made from renewable resources such as municipal solid waste and biomass crops. Methanol is a simple alcohol, often used as a racing fuel. It's used with a catalyst such as NaOH or KOH to make biodiesel. Methanol absorbs water from the air, so containers of it should be kept closed tightly, and users should purchase methanol that's known to be dry (anhydrous) or is 99.9 percent pure.

METHOXIDE—In biodiesel production, "methoxide" is a commonly used term for the product of mixing methanol and sodium hydroxide, a product that will produce its own heat through an exothermic reaction. If it splashes on you, rinse with water and seek medical attention immediately. It's also highly corrosive. Making methoxide is the most dangerous step when making biodiesel. Carefully consider the safety of the design of your equipment and workspace before producing, and always wear protective clothing and a respirator when handling. Use methoxide immediately, as it loses its reactive properties over time.

MISCIBILITY—A chemistry term that refers to the ability of liquids to mix easily in all proportions.

MONOGLYCERIDES—*See* diglycerides.

NaOH—The chemical term for sodium hydroxide, also known as lye or caustic soda.

pH—A measure of acidity and alkalinity of a solution on a scale, with 7 being neutral. Lower numbers indicate increasing acidity, while higher numbers indicate increasing alkalinity.

RAPESEED—A plant in the mustard family that produces a food-grade oil that can either be further processed into canola oil or be used in its raw form. Can be used to make biodiesel.

SAPONIFICATION—Usually, a process by which triglycerides are reacted with sodium or potassium hydroxide to produce glycerol and a fatty acid salt, called "soap." In simpler terms, it generally refers to making soap, which we do when making biodiesel, but which we want to limit as much as possible.

SOY—Also called soy oil, a vegetable oil pressed from soybeans. Soy is currently the most common virgin oil source for biodiesel in the U.S. Rapeseed is more common in other countries.

SVO—Acronym for "straight vegetable oil." SVO is used cooking oil that has been filtered to about 1 micron to allow it to be used as a fuel in a diesel engine (once it has been heated). SVO and WVO are similar, but different in that SVO is filtered, whereas WVO is the used oil unfiltered.

TITRATION—Basically, a test for FFAs (free fatty acids) in waste restaurant fryer oil.

TRANSESTERIFICATION—Process of making biodiesel by adding an alcohol (such as methanol), plus a base of either lye or KOH, to used oil to convert it into biodiesel and glycerine.

TRIGLYCERIDE—A naturally occurring ester of three fatty acids and glycerol that is the chief constituent of fats and oils.

VISCOSITY—A liquid's resistance to flow. Sometimes thought of as its thickness or thinness. Methanol has a low viscosity (easily flows), while vegetable oil has a high viscosity (flows more slowly, with greater resistance).

WASTE OIL HEATER—A heater used for heating living spaces that burns waste oil products. Some will burn any type of waste oil, including motor oil, cooking oil, transmission fluid, or hydraulic fluid. (See the Resources section for vendors.)

WVO—Acronym for "waste vegetable oil." WVO is the usual starting product for the making of biodiesel, but is also used in SVO systems. WVO refers to used, unfiltered oil. For biodiesel we only filter to about 600 microns as the smaller particles will settle out in the process, therefore we're using WVO (essentially dirty oil, as 600 microns does little to clarify it). SVO users must take the WVO, which is very dirty, and filter it down to about 1 micron before they can use it straight, in a diesel engine (after heating), leaving it much clearer and purer than the starting WVO.

COLD-WEATHER TEST LOGBOOK

Make copies of this sheet and use them to do your cold-weather testing.

Sample #	Blend	Date	Temperature	Results
1				
2				
3				
4				
5				
6				
7				
8				
9				
10				

KOH Titration Calculator

To calculate titration, first read the gallons of oil you're using in the top row. Then use the titration number in the following rows to cross-reference the intersection—the result is the grams of KOH you use. Valid only for 90 percent pure KOH. All other purities of KOH must use the biodiesel calculator referenced in the Resources section. We are also calculating this using a base amount of 7 g of KOH, as that is a popular amount and has worked well for us (proven in testing).

Titration Number	Gallons of Oil						
	20	30	40	50	60	70	80
0.25	610	915	1220	1525	1830	2135	2439
0.50	631	946	1262	1577	1893	2208	2524
0.75	652	978	1304	1630	1956	2282	2608
1.00	673	1009	1346	1682	2019	2355	2692
1.25	694	1041	1388	1735	2082	2429	2776
1.50	715	1073	1430	1788	2145	2503	2860
1.75	736	1104	1472	1840	2208	2576	2944
2.00	757	1136	1514	1893	2271	2650	3028
2.25	778	1167	1556	1945	2334	2723	3112
2.50	799	1199	1598	1998	2397	2797	3197
2.75	820	1230	1640	2050	2461	2871	3281
3.00	841	1262	1682	2103	2524	2944	3365
3.25	862	1293	1724	2156	2587	3018	3449
3.50	883	1325	1767	2208	2650	3091	3533
3.75	904	1356	1809	2261	2713	3165	3617
4.00	925	1388	1851	2313	2776	3239	3701
4.25	946	1420	1893	2366	2839	3312	3785
4.50	967	1451	1935	2418	2902	3386	3870
4.75	988	1483	1977	2471	2965	3459	3954
5.00	1009	1514	2019	2524	3028	3533	4038
5.25	1030	1546	2061	2576	3091	3607	4122
5.50	1052	1577	2103	2629	3155	3680	4206
5.75	1073	1609	2145	2681	3218	3754	4290
6.00	1094	1640	2187	2734	3281	3827	4374
6.25	1115	1672	2229	2786	3344	3901	4458

SHOPPING LIST WORKSHEET

Make copies of this sheet and use them to help with your shopping.

Qty.	Item Description & Notes	Part # or Size	Vendor	Cost
			Grand Total	

SAMPLE PARTS LIST

If you will be building your own cone bottom processor, this list will get you started. This is just a very basic starter list. The book will guide you through some of the other items needed.

Qty.	Part Type	Size	Notes
	Ball valves	$3/4$''	brass
	Hose	$3/4$''	reinforced vinyl, heavy wall
	Hose clamps	$3/4$''–$1^1/4$''	
	Fuel filter and housing	$3/4$''	10 micron filter or finer
	Motor wiring		
	4-hour timer for processor pump		Intermatic brand
	Electrical box		Exterior w/ $3/4$'' threaded openings
	Mist washing setup		
	Aquarium air stone		bubble washing items
	Aquarium air pump		bubble washing items
	Air hose for bubbler		bubble washing items
	MDPE conical tank & stand	60 gallon	for main reactor
	MDPE conical tank & stand	15 gallon	for methoxide mixer
	Processing pump	1 inch	720 gph is best
	Oil heating setup		
	Oil collection setup		
	Fuel drying setup		
	Poly barrels		for storing fuel, oil, etc.
	Steel barrels		for collecting oil at restaurants, heating oil, etc.
	Goggles		safety gear
	Respirator		safety gear
	Chemically resistant gloves		safety gear
	Safety apron		safety gear
	Scale		accurate to 0.1 g for titrations
	Scale		accurate to 1 g for making larger batches

1. David Goodstein, *Out of Gas: The End of the Age of Oil* (New York: Norton, 2005).

2. KSBW TV news report, Salinas, California, August 20, 2007.

3. Wadi'h Halabi, "Capitalism Incapable of Reversing Environmental Crisis," *People's Weekly World Newspaper*, May 17, 2007.

4. Quoted in Albert A. Bartlett, "Thoughts on Long-term Energy Supplies: Scientists and the Silent Lie," *Physics Today*, July 2004.

5. Halabi.

6. Ibid.

7. E. M. Morrison, "Biodiesel Goes Off-road," *AG Innovation News*, April–June 2006.

8. Pacific Biodiesel website, *www.biodiesel.com/theFuel.htm*.

9. "Global Warming by the Numbers: Challenge Is Clear for the New Congress," *Environmental Defense*, January 16, 2007.

10. Ibid.

11. Ibid.

12. "References for Great Lakes Statistics," U.S. Environmental Protection Agency and AskNumbers.com; *www.asknumbers.com/VolumeConversion.aspx*.

13. Paul Thompson, *The Beginner's Guide to Peak Oil: How Peak Oil Could Lead to Starvation*, The Wolf at the Door, *www.wolfatthedoor.org.uk*.

14. Ibid.

15. Tim Appenzeller, "The End of Cheap Oil," *National Geographic*, June 2004.

16. Walter Youngquist and Richard C. Duncan, "North American Natural Gas: Data Show Supply Problems," *Natural Resource Research*, 2003; vol. 12, p. 229.

17. Carola Hoyos, "Study Sees Harmful Hunt for Extra Oil," *Financial Times*, February 12, 2007.

18. Ibid.

19. "Thoughts on Long-term Energy Supplies."

20. Cheryl Woodard, "Facing the End of Oil," AskQuestions.org, February 16, 2005.

21. Ibid.

22. Tom Whipple, "Peak Oil Review," Association for the Study of Peak Oil and Gas, July 9, 2007.

23. "Africa's Huge Oil Project a Boondoggle?" *Environmental Defense*, June 24, 2002.

24. "Peak Oil Review." *www.aspo-usa.com/index.php?option=com_content&task= view&id=167&Itemid=91*.

25. Peak Oil Hearing: Udall Testimony, December 7, 2005, *www.globalpublicmedia.com/ transcripts/587*.

26. Udall Testimony.

27. "Facing the End of Oil."

28. "BioFuels: What's Down the Road for Motorists? Biofuels!" *www.CarJunky.com*, March 9, 2007.

29. Ibid.

30. E. M. Morrison, "Chow Down: High Corn Prices and Abundant Biofuel Coproducts Spark Interest in Feed-corn Substitutes," *AG Innovation News*, July–September 2007.

31. "BioFuels: Environmental Pros and Cons of Switching to Plant-based Bio-fuels," *www.CarJunky.com*, February 17, 2007.

32. "Chow Down."

33. "BioFuels: What's Down the Road for Motorists? Biofuels!"

34. "Energy Efficiency and Renewable Energy Biomass Program: Renewable Diesel Fuel," U.S. Department of Energy.

35. Ibid.

36. "BioFuels: What's Down the Road for Motorists? Biofuels!"

37. "Energy Efficiency and Renewable Energy Biomass Program: Ethanol," U.S. Department of Energy.

38. Ibid.

39. Scott Faber, "The Ruminant: Fertile Ground," *Environmental Defense*, July 6, 2007.

40. Ibid.

41. "BioFuels: What's Down the Road for Motorists? Biofuels!"

42. "Energy Efficiency and Renewable Energy Biomass Program: Ethanol."

43. "BioFuels: Environmental Pros and Cons."

44. "BioFuels: What's Down the Road for Motorists? Biofuels!"

45. Pacific Biodiesel website, *www.biodiesel.com/theFuel*.htm.

46. "Energy Efficiency and Renewable Energy Biomass Program."

47. "BioFuels: Environmental Pros and Cons."

48. Anthony Radich: "Biodiesel Performance, Cost, and Use," *www.eia.doe.gov/oiaf/analysispaper/biodiesel/index.html*.

49. "Gasoline and Diesel Fuel Update," U.S. Department of Energy, Energy Information Administration.

50. TractorByNet.com bulletin board, *www.tractorbynet.com/forums/showthread.php?p=1210453*.

51. Jeffrey Yago, Backwoods Home Magazine, *www.backwoodshome.com/articles2/yago101.html*.

52. "Alternative Fuel Vehicles: New ATV Takes Fuel Efficiency to New Levels," *www.CarJunky.com*.

53. "Energy Efficiency and Renewable Energy Biomass Program: Renewable Diesel Fuel."

54. "Biodiesel Goes Off-road."

55. "Chow Down."

56. Pacific Biodiesel website.

57. *www.tuningnews.net/article.php/date=061101c*.

58. Xanterra Parks and Resorts website, *www.xanterra.com*.

59. National Biodiesel board, *www.biodiesel.org*.

60. For more information on EPAct, go to the EPAct website at *www1.eere.energy.gov/vehiclesandfuels/epact/about/epact_fuels.html*.

61. Go to *www1.eere.energy.gov/vehiclesandfuels/epact/about/epact*.

62. *www.cumminsracing.com*.

63. Troy from the Biodiesel Collaborative website at *www.biodieselcommunity.org*.

64. From the EPA website, *www.epa.gov/otaq/consumer/08-fire.pdf*.

65. Jeffrey G. Rothermel, "Investigation of Transesterification Reaction Rates and Engine Exhaust Emissions of Biodiesel Fuels," thesis, Iowa State University, 2003.

66. Posted by High Compression II at *http://biodiesel.infopop.cc/groupee/forum*.

INDEX